UnBreakable

—— an interactive guide ——

★ ★ ★

Praise for *UnBreakable*

"This is no stuffy, wordy, boring marriage book! The stories, authors' real life experience, and easy-to-read content make it great for the reluctant partner. Here you will not only learn about healthy relationships—you will be challenged to live them out. Many couples and small groups will be strengthened by this work."
—Laura Demetrician, LMF, spiritual director, marriage and family therapist

"*UnBreakable* is a field-tested manual—a superb blend of biblical truth, practical wisdom, and personal application. If you want to go beyond a marriage that merely survives but actually thrives, this excellent resource is for you. And while you're at it, grab a few extra copies and dive in with other couples in a group setting. More joy and togetherness lie ahead!"
—Quintin Stieff, lead pastor, Valley Church, West Des Moines, IA

"Married couples often tell me their marriage is so broken, they don't know if it can be repaired. *UnBreakable* is a fresh, thought-provoking, simple study guide for married couples living in a complicated, overworked, overcommitted world. These practical and doable solutions can help to repair what is broken."
—Sheila Stone Chapman, psychotherapist, author of *Drive Thru Couple's Counseling*

"*UnBreakable* is a practical, interactive guide and brings the prospect of contentment and delight back within reach for marriages that may be on the brink. Particularly poignant are the "True Confessions" of the authors and their wives, highlighting the visceral realities and stressors threatening even the best marriages of our day. I commend *UnBreakable* to all generations, at all levels of marital maturity, for preventative or remedial measures. I also recommend it for those involved in mentoring or facilitating couples' discipleship."
—Tom Mouw, superintendent, North Central District, Evangelical Free Church of America

"After over thirty-five years of ministry, it's exciting to find this new resource and to anticipate the blessing it will be to couples and those who work with them. Charles and Tony have created a workbook that is both engaging and challenging, providing a tool that invites and empowers partners to share honestly and openly as they deepen and enrich their relationship. Using personal stories and probing questions, the authors have provided a highly relatable workbook that will benefit both married and soon-to-be married couples. We are looking forward to the positive impact their work will have on couples in our ministry."
—Mike Slaughter, lead pastor, Ginghamsburg Church
Carolyn Slaughter, director of marriage preparation, Ginghamsburg Church

CharlesCausey & TonyMiltenberger

UnBreakable
—— an interactive guide ——
★ ★ ★

Forging a Marriage of Contentment and Delight

Abingdon Press

Nashville

UNBREAKABLE:
FORGING A MARRIAGE OF CONTENTMENT AND DELIGHT

This book is printed on acid-free paper.

ISBN 978-1-4267-8435-4

Scripture quotations unless noted otherwise are from the Common English Bible. Copyright © 2011 by the Common English Bible. All rights reserved. Used by permission. www.CommonEnglishBible .com.

Scripture quotations marked "NKJV™" are taken from the New King James Version®. Copyright © 1982 by Thomas Nelson, Inc. Used by permission. All rights reserved.

Scripture quotations marked (NASB) are taken from the New American Standard Bible®, Copyright © 1960, 1962, 1963, 1968, 1971, 1972, 1973, 1975, 1977, 1995 by The Lockman Foundation. Used by permission. (www.Lockman.org)

Disclaimer: Names and identifying details in this book have been changed to protect the identities of the couples.

14 15 16 17 18 19 20 21 22 23 — 10 9 8 7 6 5 4 3 2 1

MANUFACTURED IN THE UNITED STATES OF AMERICA

To Lauri and Karen

Contents

Contents

Introduction

We believe humans become adults when they are capable of real love. Until we are capable of loving someone deeply and authentically, we live in a state of emotional deficit and we project to others a sense of need. When our love is shallow, it is easy to presume we know what the other person is thinking and feeling. When our love is shallow, we tend to put others down, mistakenly believing that it will somehow elevate us. Mature adults in deep and authentic loving relationships, however, lift others up. They cease to focus on their own needs and focus more on the needs of others.

What is real love? God is love. This is the single most important truth in the universe. This love of God is utterly disassociated with need. God is complete and self-sufficient. *Being* love, God desires to *give* love. This is what is so different from what we see in relationships today.

For most humans, love is about getting rather than giving. This turns God-designed love on its head. This human, self-oriented love strips the power from the love God designed for us to share with one another. The power of love rests in its ability to give unconditionally, as God gives love and as God intends for us to give love.

UnBreakable aims to guide couples to develop this other-oriented, God-designed love, which we see as a bottomless pool of revitalizing and thirst-quenching love. This kind of love communicates to others that they are more important than anything.

We are swimming in a society with mediocre images of marriage. Much of what we see in relationships today is not love but the craving to be loved. Since most say love is the answer, our questions are: What does it mean when we tell someone, "I love you"? What does it look like to love deeply, authentically? Our goal in writing *UnBreakable* is for the reader to develop clear answers to these questions, coupled with passion, to experience a legendary love with his or her spouse.

A Few Notes about the Book and Our Perspective

Our primary experience vocationally is as part of the military. This roots us in a particular point of view and shapes the stories we tell and the issues we address. However, we hope this resource provides help and renewal not just for military couples but for all married couples.

It is important to note one basic assumption we make in this book: that marriage is defined, for us personally and for the purposes of the book, in the traditional biblical and heterosexual sense. This is the point of view from which we have experience and thus is the point of view from which we write.

Finally, and most importantly, we want to be clear about another assumption. We are writing here for couples that are experiencing mild to moderate conflict or other issues in their marriages and for couples who simply wish to improve their marriages. We are *not* addressing couples who are experiencing abuse or severe conflict of any kind. We cannot state it strongly enough: *If you are experiencing violence or abuse, either as victim or as perpetrator, you must seek professional help, a safe house, and the assistance of law enforcement.*

How to Use This Book

We strongly encourage couples to work through this book and its exercises in a group setting with a trained facilitator.

Each of the *UnBreakable* workbook sessions is laid out into seven sections:

I. Background Story

This section will contain a story about a couple struggling with married life and identifying if they really love their mate and if their mate loves them. The names and identifying details in these stories have been changed.

II. Going Deeper

This is a chance to look under the surface and see what the biblical principles are and to reflect on the issues a couple might be facing. You will hear, alternatively, from each author (Charles and Tony) and our wives (Lauri and Karen). This section can be used either in a small-group study or as a personal devotional. This section includes the following:

The Scriptures
The Principle
Arrows on Target
True Confessions
Prayer

III. Individual Journal Questions

This section is meant to be done alone during an individual's devotional time.

IV. Couple Interactive Exercise(s)

This section is specifically designed for a couple to do together on a date night or when they have an hour to enjoy together.

V. Couple Questions for Date Night

This section is also to be looked at together as a couple on a date night or during a couple meeting time.

VI. Small-Group Study and Discussion Questions
   This section is designed for small groups and their leaders.

VII. Unbreakable Challenge
   This section includes an assignment designed to challenge couples and to provide practice in working together as a partnership.

Foundations

Then God said, "Let us make humanity in our image to resemble us so that they may take charge of the fish of the sea, the birds in the sky, the livestock, all the earth, and all the crawling things on earth."
God created humanity in God's own image,
  in the divine image God created them,
    male and female God created them.
God blessed them and said to them, "Be fertile and multiply; fill the earth and master it. Take charge of the fish of the sea, the birds in the sky, and everything crawling on the ground."

—Genesis 1:26-28

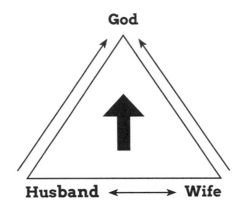

Main Point

God made humankind to mirror God's image here on earth. God made two different kinds of humans, male and female, so they would (as a couple) reflect God's image and likeness. Besides being image bearers, God wants couples to be fruitful and multiply a godly heritage. Also, God wants humans to be good stewards over creation.

Since God made marriage, God is to remain an integral part of the couple's life together. As you see in the diagram (above), as a husband and wife move closer to God, they move closer together. Also, as the couple moves closer together, they find themselves closer to God.

I. Background Story

Jim and Kelly have been married nine years and had two boys. They lived in a beautiful home with a heavy mortgage. Jim wasn't exactly an athlete, but he wasn't a slouch either; he worked out three times a week to fight off the spare-tire look. Kelly, on the other hand, was a natural beauty. Kelly's dark hair and skin tone made her attractive, especially to Jim.

Their marriage was not quite a storybook romance, but they believed they loved each other. For years Jim bought Kelly flowers, chocolate, and jewelry at just the right times, when she was feeling down or needed to be reminded of his love. Kelly always appreciated these thoughtful reminders, yet wished Jim would think of helping her more in the ordinary things of life, like with rearing the young boys.

Since the kids had gotten older, and Jim worked longer hours, his romantic gestures dwindled, and the rare times they had to spend alone as a couple became mundane. People on the outside couldn't tell, but they were beginning to have more stress, arguments, and isolation from each other instead of working together as a team. Many times their conversations were sprinkled with anger that led to evenings of avoidance. Even their faith, which was once an integral part of their relationship together, had now become just a mere sixty minutes at church on Saturday night.

One night in the bedroom, as they were preparing to turn out the lights, Kelly decided to say something to Jim about their relationship.

"Are we okay?" Kelly asked pleasantly.

"What do you mean?" Jim responded with a look of panic on his face. He re-arranged his posture to face Kelly, as if preparing for the worst.

"Well, I just feel like we're not connecting much anymore," said Kelly. "We say 'I love you' to each other, but what does that mean? Lately it just seems like something to say."

That stung Jim a little, but he tried to bury it. "Are you sure you want to have this conversation tonight?" Jim asked as he turned off his bedside lamp and slipped his feet into the sheets.

"I'm not sure, Jim, but I am sure I don't want to wake up ten years from now, with the boys out of the home, and not know each other anymore," Kelly said as she laid down next to him.

"I think you're thinking about things too much, Kelly. I mean, ten years is a long time away. I try to just worry about tomorrow's issues."

"I'm sorry for bringing this up before we go to bed, but I look at our friends' marriages and they don't seem happy either. Not like when we were just married. Do you remember those first three years before we had kids and would go on walks in the park? I want that magic again."

Neither one said a word after that. Kelly soon fell asleep, but Jim lay awake staring at the dark ceiling. He was thinking about all of the things he had said, and hadn't said, to Kelly during the week before.

II. Going Deeper

The Scriptures

"This is the reason that a man leaves his father and mother and embraces his wife, and they become one flesh. The two of them were naked, the man and his wife, but they weren't embarrassed." (Genesis 2:24-25)

"Two are better than one because they have a good return for their hard work. If either should fall, one can pick up the other. But how miserable are those who fall and don't have a companion to help them up!" (Ecclesiastes 4:9-10)

"God is the one who enables you both to want and to actually live out his good purposes." (Philippians 2:13)

The Principle

When God created Adam and Eve, marriage was instituted as a fundamental relationship, a building block of society. In marriage, a couple leaves their parents and becomes a separate entity. The "we" and "us" then become stronger than the "you" and "me" components. This union is an intellectual, emotional, physical, and spiritual unity. Our definition of marriage is one man and one woman in a one-flesh relationship for one lifetime.

Arrows on Target

Jim and Kelly are struggling over something very typical to married couples— wondering if their love is a love of a lifetime. It is common in marriage with all the responsibilities and work of raising a family to let your primary relationship slip some. In every relationship the warm, fuzzy feelings of love only last for a short period of time, two to three years at most. Familiarity begins to breed contempt, and then we see each other for who we really are.

Remember, marriage is not the place where one gets completed as a person. It is a place where complete persons come together and build a "we" that is bigger and better than either one of the "I"s. Many people see marriage as a shortcut to completeness or a meaningful life. These people marry in naiveté and soon realize marriage is hard, requiring strength to find the right measure of love and commitment to honor your spouse and complement, rather than complete, him or her.

When you committed your life to your mate, you made a sacred vow to cherish and honor him or her for the rest of your life. God takes this very seriously. It is imperative to understand how to love your spouse with an unbreakable love, and the next few chapters will teach you this.

True Confessions

(Lauri speaking) I sometimes understand why people get divorced. Looking back, there were several periods in our twenty-one years together when things were very difficult for me. Charles has a problem with overcommitting to things. With a full-time job, he will add on another full-time job or two degree programs simultaneously or commit his time to ministries and people until he has none available for the family. Simply said, he puts too much on his plate, and then I have to be the bad guy and tell him he has to drop something. There have been several rough eras when I didn't think we would make it through. There have also been good eras. When we were first married and without children, Charles and I lived in Lincoln, Nebraska. We would take long walks on a college campus across the street. They had a dairy store, so we walked on the trails and ate ice cream together. Those were good days for us because we invested casual time in our relationship. When Charles overcommits, he robs our relationship of time together, and he doesn't seem to care about it. That is what is so irritating to me. Yet, I have overcome these feelings with the knowledge that Charles and I are a team and will be together for a lifetime. I don't consider divorce to be an option for me. In my marriage, which is full of the normal ups and downs, divorce is just not something I consider. This is one thing that has gotten us through the stressful times. All in all, I believe in what Charles does; I just want him to remember he is part of a relationship and not to forget about me.

Prayer

Lord, you are the creator of all things good, including the marriage relationship. Please help me understand your plan and purpose for my life. Help me honor you with my life and commit myself to your plans and not my own. Please forgive me for the times I have rejected my spouse and was bitter. Please help me love my mate deeply. Please give me the assurance and strength I need to go the distance. Help us as a couple see your role in our relationship and realize that as we individually draw closer to you, we will find ourselves closer to each other. Help us understand that this is our greatest good.

III. Individual Journal Questions

1. Knowing that God created marriage and purposely brought you and your mate together, write down ideas about how you know for certain you were supposed

to be together. (Hint: Think of instances you had no control over but during which God used your mate to help you, or think of the providential way God brought you together.)

2. What is the greatest strength in your marriage? What are some ways your spouse's personality makes you laugh?

3. In Genesis 2 it says that the husband and wife will become one flesh. Besides physical intimacy, what are ways you have become one with your spouse?

4. Think of your marriage like a garden. What areas are doing well right now, and what areas need some weeding, watering, and attention?

IV. Couple Interactive Exercises

Unbreakable Skill #1: "The Responsibility Skill"

—I am 100% responsible for how I think, feel, and act.

—In my relationship I am 100% responsible *to* love, support, and communicate with my spouse.

Sometimes it is easier to blame your spouse than to take responsibility for your own actions. Here are three parts to the responsibility skill that will help you in your marriage:

A. Taking responsibility means that you will do an assessment of yourself in every situation and ask yourself, "What role did I play in this argument?" Or, "How was I at fault?" Or, "What do I need to do to make this better?" One of the ways that we suggest couples start taking responsibility is by using "I" statements. "I" statements remind all of us that we had a part to play in the argument or discussion. "I" statements also force us to take a look at the emotional truth in the situation. For example, "You always ignore my grocery list." Changed to an "I" statement looks like, "I feel like the grocery list I put together gets ignored." The tone in the two sentences is drastically different, and when you are trying to talk about the tough stuff, it will make all the difference in the world.

B. Understanding responsibility in marriage will also relieve you of the pressure of being responsible *for* your spouse's feelings. Too often we get wrapped up into thinking that it is our job to make our spouse feel complete. There is danger in that thinking; it neglects the importance of our own feelings and disregards the importance of God's work in each of our lives. When we begin to understand that we aren't responsible for our spouses' emotions (i.e., making them happy), then we can move forward to truly serve them the way Christ serves us.

C. You are responsible to love, support, and communicate with your spouse. While you aren't responsible for his or her emotional response, you do have a role to play in marriage. The minute you begin to neglect that role, what you are really saying is that you aren't 100 percent committed to your marital vows. Understanding that you have to be in the trenches with your spouse is a great way to open things up in your relationship and push through difficulties.

To summarize:
Use "I" statements instead of "you" statements.
You are responsible *to* your spouse, but not *for* him or her.
Always communicate with your spouse to persevere through tough conflicts.

Exercise #1

Write down what specific experiences, gifts, talents, strengths, and abilities you and your spouse bring into the relationship to form a partnership (if you can only come up with a few, think about mental, physical, spiritual, or social strengths):

My Spouse	**Me**
_____	_____
_____	_____
_____	_____
_____	_____
_____	_____

Exercise #2

Exchange workbooks. Write a short love note to your spouse in his or her book. (Hint: When writing, try to complete these two statements: The part of your personality that attracts me the most is_____. Your relationship with God encourages me spiritually by_____.)

V. Couple Questions for Date Night

1. Read over exercise #1 together and what each of you wrote down regarding strengths. Discuss which items were similar and dissimilar.

2. Discuss how you can make the marriage one with more complementing than completing.

3. In the story about Jim and Kelly, in what ways can you relate to their discussion about love and magic? In what ways is your relationship different?

4. Share and discuss the love letter you wrote for your spouse in exercise #2. Verbalize to your mate any items that need to be discussed. Close in prayer, thanking God for each other.

VI. Small-Group Study and Discussion Questions

1. **Open** in prayer.

2. **Ask:** What is the greatest thing about being married?

3. **Read** out loud the background story.

4. **Ask:** In what ways is your marriage like Jim and Kelly's?

5. **Read** Ecclesiastes 4:9-10 and Genesis 2:24-25.

6. **Ask:** In what ways has being married lifted you up spiritually, emotionally, physically, or socially? How has being married given you a good return for your labor? From the Genesis passage, how is it that married couples can be considered one flesh? In what ways do a husband and wife form one entity? What level of transparency should accompany this type of closeness?

7. **Review** the "True Confessions" section. Have you ever felt the way Lauri did? What did you do about it?

8. **Read** Philippians 2:13. How have you seen God at work in your marriage?

9. **Close** in prayer after asking if anyone else has something they would like to share about their marriage with the group.

VII. Unbreakable Challenge

Have a couple meeting and bring your calendars along. In the next six weeks, plan out three couple meetings (that can be done at home) for at least an hour, and plan out three dates (that must be done away from home). The couple meetings are times to do your exercises together and review the workbook material as you go through it. The dates are for your personal enjoyment, and you should talk about anything except the hard issues (save those for couple meetings). The more you put into your marriage the more you will get out of it. We are challenging you to throw the ball deep and create a love relationship that will withstand the test of time.

Also, each week we will ask you to summarize what you are learning in a promise statement. At the end of the book we will ask you to summarize the seven promise statements into a Marriage Mission Statement. Here is your first opportunity to write down a promise in a response to the section on foundations.

Develop a marriage promise statement for foundations by filling in the blank below:

*I promise that I will*_____

_____.

Session Two

Unbreakable Love Concept #1— Commitment

*Above all, keep fervent in your love for one another,
because love covers a multitude of sins.*

—1 Peter 4:8 NASB

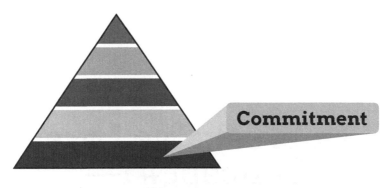

Main Point

Commitment is the action of your loyalty. It is an indicator that you are a person of integrity—or not. You gave your word that you would accept your spouse no matter what. Your word is your life; you live or die by it, rise or fall with it.

I. Background Story

Ray and Sylvia had been married twelve years. They had two young children, and life seemed pretty full. Ray worked hard at his job as a defense contractor, and Sylvia was a professor at the local business college. When they were courting and just after their marriage, it was easy to connect. They had some very romantic dates followed by warm evenings sitting by a fire. Recently, however, they just couldn't seem to connect.

Ray's work seemed to keep him later and later causing suppertime to be delayed or eaten separately. Ray seemed more preoccupied, yet nagged Sylvia about the details of life. Sylvia felt isolated from Ray, and as she poured her life more into the children, saw Ray increasingly as an appendage to the family.

One night the two had gone on a date to pull things together but had barely spoken a word while eating. They drove from the restaurant to their home in silence, both deep in thought. The car pulled into the driveway, and the couple was glad the boys' bedroom lights were off, which meant the children were already in bed. Neither one reached for the car door handles when Ray pushed the ignition button and the car quieted.

Finally, Sylvia broke the silence, "Ray, I just want to say, I know I have caused you some consternation lately regarding our relationship. But, well, I want you to know I appreciate the times like tonight when you make an effort for us to be together."

"Thanks, honey." Ray reached over and grabbed Sylvia's hand.

Sylvia continued, "I know I'm not perfect, but there have been times when you seem in your own world lately and act like you don't need me, and it really bugs me. There are times when you say you're listening and I know you're not, and I want to shake you because I get so mad. There are times when we argue and you seem so self-confident, almost cocky, as if your ideas can't ever be wrong, but you are wrong sometimes."

"You forgot to mention how sometimes I side with the boys when you are arguing with one of them—"

"Yes! That, too, irritates me. Even interrupting me just now bugs me. It's like you're telling me you know how to communicate what I think better than I do," said Sylvia.

"No, I didn't mean to do that," said Ray.

"I know, but it comes out that way."

There was a moment of silence while both of them realized their conversation had gotten very deep and sensitive. They hadn't had time for an uninterrupted conversation for a while, and it seemed Sylvia needed a moment to pour out her thoughts.

Sylvia seemed to always air her frustrations without asking Ray what his might be. Ray was glad to finally be getting closer to the issues that might be bothering Sylvia.

"Is there anything else, honey?" Ray asked.

"Yes, there is."

"Well, do you want to talk about it?"

"I don't know," replied Sylvia.

"Why not?"

"Because it's stuff that really bothers me, but I'm realizing while I'm sitting here that you may never change. I just may have to accept you for who you are."

Ray smiled a little, "Well, that sounds pretty good."

Sylvia shook her head.

Ray could tell she was starting to fume. He did not want to be flippant when Sylvia was serious. He just had a hard time sometimes not laughing with nervous energy when Sylvia expressed dissatisfaction. This always made her more upset, so Ray tried not to smile and looked down at the steering wheel, then to their interlocked hands.

"Ray, I guess we just need to go inside. Otherwise this could get more serious and—"

"And what?"

"Well, I don't want us to get into a big fight tonight. Our marriage could be worse; at least we are still together."

"For now," said Ray slowly.

"What do you mean?" asked Sylvia.

"Look, Sylvia, I know I'm not perfect either, but it's pretty easy to see that you would rather be somewhere else or with someone else most of the time. I would really like to get to the bottom of what's troubling you."

"Not tonight," Sylvia said forcefully.

"Fine," Ray said with some edge to his voice.

"There you go again, pouting. I don't like that about you. You use guilt to get me to do things I don't want to do."

"No, I don't," said Ray, then thought about it a second. "Do I?"

"Yes, you do, and it's a habit. You're like a little boy sometimes."

Ray became very agitated with this comment because he felt like Sylvia wasn't respecting him very much. He worked hard to help provide for the family; he made sacrifices so she could have the house she wanted and the things she needed, but then, for thanks, he was mocked. He was going to shout back something ugly, but he reminded himself that he loved her, and though she was criticizing him and being unfair, there was another issue that was deeper, and it was inside Sylvia.

"Ray, we've grown apart. We don't do things for fun anymore, and that's what I need. I need you to want me for things outside of the bedroom."

"What do you mean?" Ray asked. He was glad the conversation had deescalated some.

"Well, like time with your bowling buddies. I don't want you to quit the Sunday ritual with them, but you and I don't have something like that where we look forward to it all week and spend recreational time together and laugh and catch up. Why can't we have some fun, frivolous time together where we play and relax?"

"We can," Ray responded.

"But you don't ever plan it."

"We've had fun together before."

"Ray, you don't treat me as a friend who you want to plan fun things with. I feel more like an object sometimes or a useful apparatus for you to enjoy whenever you want. I'm not a vending machine."

"I—"

Ray started to answer but then nothing he was going to say seemed connected to what Sylvia was commenting on. He wanted to talk about their love life and how Sylvia might improve herself there, but the conversation had shifted, and now it was about him keeping their marriage fun. He also realized she hadn't asked him what *he* thought might be issues in their marriage. *Marriage is too tough*, thought Ray.

"Let's just go in," said Sylvia. "We're not going to resolve anything tonight, and I'm tired and need to go to bed. Soon we'll be talking about separating."

"Okay," Ray replied, trying to say it so it would not sound like a pout.

II. Going Deeper

The Scriptures

*"Ruth replied, 'Don't urge me to abandon you, to turn back from following after you. Wherever you go, I will go; and wherever you stay, I will stay. Your people will be my people, and your God will be my God. Wherever you die, I will die, and there I will be buried. May the L*ORD *do this to me and more so if even death separates me from you.'" (Ruth 1:16-17)*

"Set me as a seal over your heart,
    as a seal upon your arm,
for love is as strong as death,

. . . .

Rushing waters can't quench love;
    rivers can't wash it away." (Song of Songs 8:6-7)

"Jesus answered, 'Haven't you read that at the beginning the creator made them male and female? And God said, "Because of this a man should leave his father and mother and be joined together with his wife, and the two will be one flesh." So they are no longer two but one flesh. Therefore, humans must not pull apart what God has put together.'" (Matthew 19:4-6)

The Principle

Commitment is the foundation of any long-lasting relationship. Commitments, vows, and promises give us security so we can be free to be ourselves and not worry about abandonment when disagreements arise. Commitment strengthens a marriage and makes it impenetrable to the fleeting stress all relationships experience. Being committed to another in a longstanding relationship displays your loyalty and trustworthiness.

Arrows on Target

God's desire is for married couples to be committed, to be Christlike, and to stay together. God's design is for all our relationships to be rooted in love. Scripture is very clear on this point. The problem is that for most, love is about getting rather than giving. This turns love on its head. Love is not this for that, *quid pro quo.* That selfish kind of love is immature and weak and holds none of the power of the deep love of God. It is shallow, fragile, and ultimately unsatisfying. The power of love rests in its ability to give unconditionally and to be committed for a lifetime.

People are often confused about what it means to be in love and, more specifically, to *love*. Sometimes, when a man says he doesn't love his wife any more, this is not really what he means; in reality, he is just not feeling the warm fuzzy feelings of being "in love." Those feeling ebb and flow, and during some periods of time you may not feel them at all. But being *out of love* is not the same as *no longer loving*. Love is an action, a choice, much more than an emotion. It is critical to remember that a couple's commitment to each other is the larger part of their love. Married couples must see this distinction so they can get over the midlife hump. Commitment, at times, is distinct from your heart; it is fact, not a feeling. It continues even when you don't feel like being married anymore.

From the background story, Ray and Sylvia need to keep divorce out of their vocabulary. Instead of imagining being with someone else, they need to look within and see the quality of love they are giving to their partner. When we cease to be takers and seek to be givers, knowing that Christ has met all of our needs on the cross, then we can truly love. Many couples stay married and remain committed despite their feelings or circumstances. They believe there is something more to be gained than to throw in the towel and abandon their relationship. Don't give up; there are greener pastures ahead.

True Confessions

(Charles speaking) I know I have an amazing wife, but when Lauri and I hit the fifteen-year mark, a heavy feeling of loneliness struck me. I thought that perhaps

Lauri was not the right one. We didn't seem to be getting along, and we were so different in our personalities. Wouldn't God want me to be with someone more like me so there could be laughter and enjoyment? Having four kids in a five-year span did not help things; at the time they were twelve, eleven, ten and seven. Our home life was chaotic, and the busyness distracted me from my primary goal of loving God and loving my wife.

What I want to say here is that I understand the thinking that your spouse is totally insane and doesn't understand you. What got me specifically through that time besides scripture was listening over and over again to C. S. Lewis's audiotapes on *The Four Loves*. I realized that what was at stake wasn't just my commitment to Lauri but also my understanding of what Christ did for me on the cross. I realized that unless I wanted to forever live a fractured life, I needed to expect less from Lauri and receive my satisfaction in the amazing love of God. I looked at what I could give instead of what I could gain. I chose commitment, and I am so grateful. Things improved from the moment I decided to commit no matter what. Sometimes we just have to be vulnerable and put ourselves out there.

Prayer

Lord, you are the most committed person in the universe. Thank you for your love and commitment to me. Please help me be a committed spouse and love my mate with my whole heart. Help me be there for him or her, even when he or she doesn't deserve it. Help me not think about the what-ifs with the exception of what I could do to improve our relationship. Help my spouse not only know how much I love him or her but also see love in my actions today. Please help me be more like you.

III. Individual Journal Questions

1. Who has the most committed marriage relationship you know of? Write about ways your relationship is alike or different from theirs.

2. What is your greatest fear in your marriage? What are some ways you might be able to overcome it?

3. First Peter 4:8 says, "Above all, show sincere love to each other, because love brings about the forgiveness of many sins." What is the greatest obstacle to loving your spouse fervently right now? This scripture claims sins can be covered over with love; what sins might your spouse have that you can love them through? What sins might you have that are being "loved" over?

4. (Reflection questions) Are you committed to completing this study with your spouse, or are you just phoning it in? Are you committed to doing the hard work in making a change in your marriage?

IV. Couple Interactive Exercise

How satisfied are you with the level of commitment you and your spouse have? Circle the number that corresponds to your answer. Draw an X through each answer you think your spouse will select.

Satisfaction with...	Low → High
Present level of commitment	1 2 3 4 5 6 7
Feeling of love when the words "I love you" are spoken to you	1 2 3 4 5 6 7
Feeling like you're going to grow old with each other	1 2 3 4 5 6 7
Commitment level vs. when you were first married	1 2 3 4 5 6 7
Ability to go deep and speak about level of commitment	1 2 3 4 5 6 7
Overall happiness with marriage	1 2 3 4 5 6 7

V. Couple Questions for Date Night

1. It may have been a few years since you have said your vows to each other. Do you still feel 100 percent committed to each other, or is something blocking the closeness in your relationship?

2. Go over the couple interactive exercise together. At which points were your guesses right regarding what your spouse might say? On which points were your guesses way off? In what area do you need to grow the most as a couple?

3. In the story about Ray and Sylvia, in what ways is your communication pattern similar to theirs? In which ways are you different? What issues do they face that are similar to your issues?

4. What are two ways you can increase commitment in your marriage relationship?

5. What is something you need to hear from your spouse on a regular basis to feel close to him or her?

VI. Small-Group Study and Discussion Questions

1. **Open** in prayer.

2. **Ask:** Who in life do you admire for having a great marriage and why?

3. **Read** out loud the background story.

4. **Ask:** In what ways is your marriage like Ray and Sylvia's?

5. **Read** Matthew 19:4-6. This is obviously a hard passage to apprehend in a society with so many divorces. However, Jesus speaks of marriage as a spiritual term, of being one flesh and never separating.

6. **Ask:** Is it merely an ideal or would it be possible for a couple getting married now to expect to stay married for a lifetime? What about after twenty years when the couple seems so distant from each other, is there hope? Is there anything you are doing today to keep your relationship dynamic and holy?

7. **Review** the "True Confessions" section. Have you ever felt the way Charles did? What did you do about it?

8. **Ask:** Is there anything holding you back from having a closer marriage with 100 percent commitment?

9. **Close** in prayer after asking if anyone else has something they would like to share with the group about commitment in their marriage.

VII. Unbreakable Challenge

Take the love vow at the end of session 7 and commit those five action steps to your mate before you go to bed tonight.

Develop a marriage promise statement for commitment by filling in the blank below:
*I promise that I will*_____ _____
_____.

Unbreakable Love Concept #2— Kindness

Love is kind.

—1 Corinthians 13:4

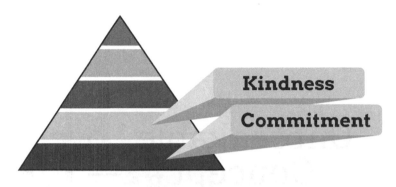

Main Point

Kindness is the volcanic core of love. Often people say they love their spouse but then are not kind to them. We saddle love up, pull the reins, and press into the stirrups, but without kindness there is no horse. You can be kind without being in love, but you cannot love without being kind. We might say we are in love (without kindness), but deep down something else abides.

I. Background Story

Mike's in-laws were in town that weekend, and he was not too happy about that. One reason for his unhappiness lay partially in the fact that they always sided with his wife, Jennifer (which was somewhat expected). The other reason was that his wife's family was always cold, so they turned up the thermostat without asking whenever they walked by it. This sounds like a minor issue, but it really irritated Mike.

Mike discovered their temperature difference when he married Jennifer six years ago. Jennifer was always cold, and Mike was always hot. At night, Jennifer added more blankets to their bed, and Mike flipped all the covers off. Jennifer placed her icy fingers and toes on Mike to warm herself up but could not stand Mike to touch her unless he ran his hands under warm water first. Jennifer could not tolerate a fan blowing on her, but Mike liked to have a fan on him all night long.

Some couples fight about finances; Mike and Jennifer fought over the room temperature, and Mike's in-laws liked to keep the house very warm. Mike dreaded visiting them because he knew he would have an awful night's sleep. He usually ended up in the basement because it was the only part of the house cool enough to sleep in. He also dreaded their visits.

On this particular visit, things were going fine, but Mike noticed that each time he glanced at the thermostat in the living room somebody had inched it up a little bit. Mike would turn it back down, not to where he liked it—on seventy—but a few degrees higher to please his in-laws.

The issue of temperature came up during supper. Jennifer's mom, Annette, declared she was too cold and wondered what they had the thermostat set at.

Mike secretly laughed at this because he figured it was she who would inch it up every so often.

"Not sure," Mike responded. "We usually keep it at about seventy in here this time of year, but I think it's on seventy-four right now."

"Well, it feels like sixty to me," Jennifer's mom said while she rubbed her arms.

Mike glanced at Jennifer and then heard, "Mike, would it kill you to turn it up a little bit while we're here? We're not used to this cooler weather." That was Jennifer's dad, Bill.

"No, Bill, it wouldn't *kill* me," Mike said sardonically. Jennifer glared at him. Annette frowned and rubbed her arms again. Bill kept eating.

"I'll go turn it up a little," Mike said as he rose from the chair.

"Thank you!" said Annette as he walked off, in a way that was not really thankful, but communicated *thanks for finally seeing it our way.*

Mike looked at the thermostat in disbelief. It was set at seventy-seven. Someone had come by just before they all sat down to eat and turned it up again. This was ridiculous. He did not know what he should do. He was already warm, but this made him even hotter. Then he heard them talking about him in the dining room.

"Is everything okay with Mike's job?" Annette asked.

"Sure, Mother, why?" asked Jennifer.

"Oh, he just seems a little irritable lately," responded Annette in more of a whisper.

"Mike's fine, Ma. No need to worry," responded Jennifer.

Mike stood there by the thermostat in the living room. He was not about to turn it up anymore, and he really didn't feel like going back into the dining area and trying to be pleasant to everyone.

"Hey, Mike, you need some help in there?" Bill asked in a mocking tone.

"Nope, just fine; be right back."

"Please raise the temp some, Mike. I think there's a draft in here," said Annette.

There's no draft in there, thought Mike. He put his finger up to the thermostat to raise it a degree but then a thought came from somewhere else that said, *Screw them.* Before he knew it, he had pushed the downward arrow button seven times putting the temperature back to his beloved seventy. Mike returned to the dining room and sat down.

"Thanks, Mike," Annette said. "What did you raise it to?"

"I actually popped it seven degrees."

"Oh, thank you," said Annette happily. "I am already feeling a little warmer."

I'll bet you are, thought Mike.

Jennifer disappeared into the kitchen forcing Mike to make small talk with Bill and Annette for a while. They were not that hard to get along with, but Mike always felt like kind of an intruder in their relationship with Jennifer. When the four of them were together, it seemed it was three against one.

"Surprise!" Jennifer said, bringing out an ice cream cake and placing it before Mike.

"What's this for?" asked Mike, thoroughly confused. He knew it wasn't his birthday or Father's Day or their anniversary. He thought, *No, it is not our anniversary.* Mike was sure.

"This was the day you came over and picked me up for our first date, and you were grilled by Daddy," Jennifer reminded him. "That was ten years ago today. This is our ten-year anniversary of being a couple." Everyone at the table was smiling at him.

"Oh, cool," Mike said, as memories started pouring into his head. "Yeah, I remember. Bill was frowning at my car and looking at my clothes and long hair curiously. That was today? I didn't remember the date, how did you—?"

Jennifer gave him a knowing smile while tapping her forehead. Then she bent down, gave Mike a nice kiss on the lips, and whispered, "I love you, honey."

"Don't you know by now, Mike, Jennifer remembers everything?" said Annette. "Always smart as a button, that one. Hey, I think I'm even colder now than I was before. What did you say you set the thermostat on?"

"Yes, I'm cold too," said Bill. "I'm going to go check it out," he said as he stood up from the table and headed toward the living room.

"Hey, no, wait a minute—!" Mike tried to scramble up and get past Jennifer quickly, a little too quickly.

"Mike, what are you doing?" Jennifer said grabbing his arm. "Daddy's just checking the thermostat. You don't need to go over there."

Mike stopped moving. "I just wanted to see—"

"See what?" asked Jennifer with a confused look on her face.

From where Mike was positioned, he could barely see Bill standing by the thermostat in the other room trying to read the numbers. Mike watched Bill reach in his shirt pocket, pull out his reading glasses, and slip them on, all while studying the thermostat.

"Hey, this thermostat is set on seventy! Somebody turned it down. I had this set on seventy-seven right before supper. Mike, I thought you said you raised the temperature seven degrees. You actually lowered it."

Mike was thinking fast. He wasn't sure how he was going to get out of this one but had to say something.

"Really? Oh, I'm sorry. I must have moved it the wrong way."

"I don't appreciate that, Mike," said Annette. "I hate being cold and uncomfortable." She got up and left the table with a very unpleasant look on her face.

Jennifer shook her head and whispered, "Mike, why are you being such a brat with my parents? I don't understand you sometimes." She left him and followed her mom into the living room.

"Eighty, that ought to do it," said Bill, sounding pleased with himself. "Hopefully this will warm things up in here a little."

Mike stood by the empty table and the melting anniversary cake, knowing that in a few minutes he would be feeling even more hot and bothered.

II. Going Deeper

The Scriptures

"What is desired in a man is kindness." (Proverbs 19:22 NKJV)

"Therefore, as God's choice, holy and loved, put on compassion, kindness, humility, gentleness, and patience." (Colossians 3:12)

"To sum up, all of you be of harmonious, sympathetic, brotherly, kindhearted, and humble in spirit; not returning evil for evil or insult for insult, but giving a blessing instead; for you were called for the very purpose that you might inherit a blessing." (1 Peter 3:8-9 NASB)

The Principle

The elemental experience of love in human relationships is kindness. A kind person is someone who is generous, patient, and compassionate. A kind person is generally warmhearted, helpful, and thoughtful. God is our example in this. God's spontaneous kindness is what reaches out from him into the human race and bestows an undeserved grace. You can be kind without being in love, but you cannot love without being kind.

Arrows on Target

After a few years, many married couples struggle with being kind to each other. A man will declare his love and commitment to his wife, even to the point of death if need be. But be kind to her on a regular basis? Forget about it.

One of the greatest and most central qualities of love is its ability to give unconditionally and without reciprocity. We see this with a mother and a baby, an altruistic friend, a loving God. With all the talk about romantic love everywhere, it is odd that this type of unconditional kindness is not seen more in marriage. Yet couples can often treat each other with a lower love than they would a neighbor, waitress, or friend.

Kindness is an act of love without expecting anything in return. One cannot earn kindness because kindness can only be given freely. In marriage we commit to be kind to our spouse whether he or she deserves it or not. Spontaneous kindness in itself, though, will elicit something when experienced. When I am kind to my spouse, it makes her feel closer to me. Kindness and closeness is what couples long for. No one wants a frigid bride or an uncaring husband.

True Confessions

(Tony speaking) When I married Karen, I didn't just marry a wonderful woman, I married her entire family, and there is a ton of them. When I say *a ton*, I want you to fully understand the definition. For example, when my oldest son had his first birthday, fifty-seven people came that were family. They were all over the place!

What that means is that every time Christmas rolls around, we have four different Christmas obligations that all seem critically important. Her family is chock-full of tradition: starting on Christmas Eve afternoon, followed by dinner on Christmas Eve, then Christmas Eve worship at 11:00 p.m., and ending the evening with the after-Christmas worship party at her grandparents' house. Yep, that is our schedule every Christmas Eve. We even have to use a "laundry basket transportation system" (patent pending) to transport the gifts back and forth to all the houses. Then, Christmas morning we get up and go see more family.

When we were first married, we even created a code word that signified when I needed a break. We called it "letting the dogs out." I would go home and literally let our two dogs out and just sit. It was glorious, and I needed it because I had never been in a family with so much tradition. My family always kept things low-key with Christmas traditions, so we just rolled with whatever was on the schedule that year. Christmas (or any holiday really) wasn't a big deal until I got married, so until then, I never knew what it meant to be busy on Christmas. The transition was difficult, and it wasn't something that I would have done on my own. If I am being honest about it, the only reason I did it was for my wife. When I said, "I do," I was also saying we would be on the same team and that her traditions were now my traditions. In some cases we do things my way, and in some cases we do things her way. Marriage is about being on the same team and doing things for your teammate. My wife has had this Christmas tradition her entire life, and there was no way that I was going to upset the apple cart because it made me uncomfortable. This wasn't about me, and the moment I made that decision is when I realized we would do this tradition every year, for as long as she wanted.

Prayer

Lord, you are the kindest person in the universe. You love and give without ceasing. Help me not take your love for granted. Help me give with the same intensity and be kind to my spouse. Help me be there and do things for him or her even when it is difficult. Please give me the strength to be kind even when my spouse is thoughtless. Help me return blessing for evil and be gracious when insulted. Please clothe me with kindness, humility, and patience.

III. Individual Journal Questions

1. Think of the ways you and your spouse have been unkind to each other during the last two weeks. Reflect on the issues. Read 1 Peter 3:8-9. Are there ways you could have been kinder and given a blessing when insulted? Write down some ideas of what you can do differently when your spouse irritates you.

2. In the story of Mike and Jennifer, what were the instances of kindness and unkindness? In what ways are you like Mike? In what ways are you more like Jennifer?

3. Is it really that hard to be kind on a regular basis? Do we lose anything by being overly kind? Think of Tony's story about Christmas—is there something in your marriage you need to be a team player about but have been resisting? Write down a couple of examples.

IV. Couple Interactive Exercises

Exercise #1

Think of four or five ways of being kind to your spouse. Write them down in the first column. Think of four or five ways your spouse could be kind to you. Write them down in the second column. Save the last couple of lines for your spouse. When both are finished, swap worksheets and allow each other to add or cross off items from the list. Plan to do at least one or two of these items this week. This shouldn't be a mechanical, wooden exercise; think of what truly pleases your mate before you write.

How I Can Be Kind to My Spouse	How My Spouse Can Be Kind to Me
_____	_____
_____	_____
_____	_____
_____	_____
_____	_____

Exercise #2

First, complete these five statements:

When you say _____ to me, it makes me feel special.

I love it when we go out to eat at _____ without the kids.

I wish we could spend more time doing (or having) _____ together.

When you ask me questions about my day, it makes me feel _____.

You are special to me because _____.

Next, read these ideas about how to be kind to your spouse. Pick one or two that you can do this week.

1. Pray and read scripture together.

2. Clean out the other's car.

3. Plan a date night and surprise your spouse by taking care of all the details (like childcare).

4. Make a special meal for your spouse.

5. Clean your stuff out of your spouse's work space.

6. Purchase something small but special that your spouse wouldn't purchase on his or her own.

7. Greet your spouse warmly when reunited at the end of the workday.

8. Frame a picture of yourself or of both of you and give it to your spouse as a gift.

9. Do your spouse's household chores while he or she is away.

10. Think of one thing that may please your spouse the most and do it soon.

11. Write a love note to your spouse and leave it under his or her pillow.

12. Tell your spouse you love him or her and why when you go to bed tonight.

V. Couple Questions for Date Night

1. Read over the fill-in-the-blank exercises from exercise #2. Are there any surprises? Discuss your answers.

2. How is the story of Mike and Jennifer like your relationship? How is it different?

3. Have you ever had a time when you really needed your spouse to be kind to you but he or she wasn't? Share with each other about this. Also, share an example of when your mate displayed unexpected kindness to you. How did it make you feel?

4. What is one way you can increase kindness in your marriage relationship?

5. Reflect on Tony's "True Confessions" story. What are some areas in your marriage where you can be better teammates (even if it doesn't involve kindness)?

VI. Small-Group Study and Discussion Questions

1. **Open** in prayer.

2. **Ask:** Why is it important to have kindness in a relationship?

3. **Read** out loud the background story.

4. **Ask:** In what ways is your marriage like Mike and Jennifer's?

5. **Read** Colossians 3:12.

6. **Ask:** What does Paul mean when he writes we need to "put on compassion, kindness, humility, gentleness, and patience" (Colossians 3:12)? Is this even possible?

7. **Review** the "True Confessions" section. What are some ways your spouse has "joined your team" and supported you even though he or she may not have wanted to? Have there been any customs or traditions in your spouse's family that you have resisted?

8. **Work together:** If you haven't completed the couple interactive exercises yet in section IV, then do them now. Did you learn anything new about your spouse in exercise #1?

9. **Ask:** What example did your parents show you regarding kindness? What side of the family do you lean toward in your own relationship?

10. **Study** Proverbs 19:22. Why is kindness desirable? (The question might seem self-evident, but is there something deeper that Solomon is saying?)

11. **Close** in prayer after asking if anyone else has something they would like to share with the group about kindness in their marriage.

VII. Unbreakable Challenge

From the second part of exercise #2 in the couple interactive exercises, pick out six items and do them all for your spouse in the next six days (one each day).

Develop a marriage promise statement for kindness by filling in the blank below:
*I promise that I will*_____
_____.

Unbreakable Love Concept #3— Honesty

Little children, let's not love with words or speech but with action and truth.

—1 John 3:18

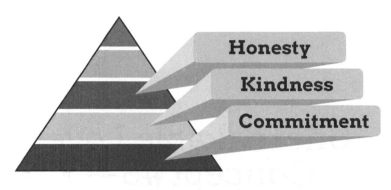

Main Point

Many couples do not have a healthy style of communication when talking about important issues. The typical conversation tends to use absolutes like "you never" and "I always." This poor communication may escalate into an argument about something that is not the root issue, turn into a chance to criticize your mate, or lead to withdrawal. These three escalations have hurt many relationships and have caused couples to avoid speaking about important issues—engaging becomes far too painful. But there is a better way.

I. Background Story

One day Julia found a receipt on Eric's dresser and decided to open it. Julia was surprised to find that it was for a new leather jacket Eric purchased for riding his motorcycle. They had been saving every month for their summer vacation, and Julia was clipping coupons and cutting corners when shopping for the family. She was pretty angry by the time Eric got home from work that night.

"So when were you going to tell me about your new motorcycle jacket?" Julia asked when Eric stepped in. "Did you think you could hide this from me?" Julia said as she waved the receipt at him.

When Eric walked in the door he was expecting a kiss, not a rebuke. He had just finished a long day at work and wasn't too happy about having to immediately go into defensive mode (and not get a kiss).

"Julia, you know I needed a new jacket, and that I've been looking online for quite a while," he responded as civilly as he could.

"Yes, I knew that, but we usually discuss purchases over two hundred dollars. Plus, I've been cutting corners so we don't go over budget each month. Do you know how many coupons it takes to save enough for that jacket?"

"No, honey, I don't, but I'm sure it's a lot." Eric moved in for a kiss, but Julia turned and walked away from him, heading for the kitchen. "Oh, so now I get the cold shoulder?" he asked.

Eric stood still in the foyer a moment, thinking of what he could say to change the subject. He made the lonely walk to his bedroom where he changed his clothes and washed his face. When he reentered the main living area, his two boys were in the kitchen and Julia was putting supper on the table. He knew they would not talk about his spending until later that evening.

When supper chores were finished and the boys were in bed, Eric and Julia found themselves on the living room sofa, each pretending to be interested in the magazine they were holding. They knew a heavy conversation was coming but didn't know who would send the first salvo.

Eric decided to launch first, "Look, Julia, you know I don't spend a lot on myself these days and I rarely shop. That jacket is really special to me, and I wasn't trying to hide it from you. I just hadn't gotten around to telling you yet."

"Eric, I also noticed you took the boys to the hunting store and bought some ammo and gear for deer season this year. We haven't even talked about you going away. Those trips cost money, and I thought we were saving for our summer vacation."

Eric was taken aback about his annual hunting trip. He thought he was through having to justify it each year. "You know I go hunting every November. What am I supposed to shoot the deer with?"

"I really don't care, but I do care that you are not very honest and open with me about our finances," Julia said.

"Now I'm being dishonest? Gee whiz, Julia, you should look in the mirror. You're the one who likes to keep secrets with your girlfriends from me and always keeps me in the dark about your family."

"What is that supposed to mean? I don't tell you things because they are told me in confidence. I don't tell you about my family because I don't want to bore you."

"Plus," Eric added, "What about the new car we got you in June? You didn't mind spending money then."

"How dare you bring up my car! You're the one who encouraged me to get it. I would have been fine with a used one, but you told me the new one was a better investment. You're the one never happy with something used."

Both of them stewed for minute over all the angry words. Julia kept shaking her head, and Eric tried to read the words on the page in front of him to no avail.

"Eric, I just want you to be honest with me and let me participate with you in our spending decisions."

"You just seem so controlling lately, Julia, and I don't like feeling henpecked in my own house. My boss messes with me at work all day, so I'd like to come home and let my hair down, not keep getting harassed."

Julia moved closer to Eric for the first time that day and put her hand on top of his. "I don't want to control you, and I know you work hard every day; so do I. I just want us to communicate better. You keep things from me, and I don't understand why. It makes me not feel loved by you."

Eric was still agitated, yet glad the conversation had eased and Julia was warming up a little. For the first time that night he thought about what was really bugging him and why he kept things from her. She was right, he knew, but he had never thought about why he was so secretive.

"Julia, I don't tell you everything because I'm afraid you're going to judge me and criticize me. I would prefer to live in peace than have to argue about everything all the time. We don't see eye to eye on a lot, and I guess in some ways I don't trust how you're going to respond. I knew you would not approve of the jacket or the hunting ammo."

"Eric, you're not giving me the benefit of the doubt. Sure, I get a little upset, but if we talk about things and I hear your reasons, I usually feel much better about your decisions. When I find receipts like the one today, it makes me think there are other things you are hiding from me—worse things—and it makes me feel uneasy."

Eric thought about Julia's last statement for a while before saying, "I think there are things both of us keep from each other. I wish—"

"You wish what?" asked Julia.

"I wish we were closer," said Eric.

II. Going Deeper

The Scriptures

"[Love] isn't happy with injustice, but it is happy with the truth." (1 Corinthians 13:6)

"By speaking the truth with love, let's grow in every way into Christ" (Ephesians 4:15)

The Principle

Jesus was the only person in human history who was full of grace and truth (John 1:14). Everyone else suffers from a disease of shallowness in both grace and truth. Truth and honesty in relationships are core components of love, just as much as commitment. Without two people being honest, there is not much of a relationship—at least not a deep one. In marriage we need to enter into the habit of speaking the unspoken truth of the situation. This is about being vulnerable and giving your mate full disclosure. We do not hide things from the one we love the most. We do not lie and shade the truth to our mate. If we truly love our spouse, we will be honest about his or her faults or our own inadequacies. If we speak the truth and are honest in a loving way, it builds a lifelong bridge of trust and commitment. Trust comes from truth. Being honest is being a grown-up Christian. Jesus was full of truth.

Arrows on Target

Open communication is vitally important to any relationship. Honesty and vulnerability in a marriage are absolute musts. When a couple begins to avoid each other because they do not see eye to eye on issues, then other areas of their relationship can crumble. Soon there might be problems with finances, children, or intimacy. Issues that affect your life together should be discussed openly.

Let your spouse hear what you are thinking. Do not be afraid to speak the truth in love. This is called compassionate truth telling. You two share the most intimate connection in life, and it is loving to be vulnerable and transparent with each other. In fact, that is part of love: no barriers, one flesh, one mind, one heart, one soul, one truth. With sex, naked bodies; with love, naked personalities.

True Confessions

(Tony speaking) I have always been the guy who wanted to fit in. I need people, and when I walk into the room everyone knows it. I like to be loud, and when I was younger I would sacrifice some of my integrity so that I could be one of the guys.

Where this played out the most was with my single friends. I got married when I was twenty-two, and I was the first person married among my peers. So when they would go out, it was all about the ladies. Now, don't get me wrong, I never went out to find a date or anything like that, but when I was on a trip to Vegas, I did something I never could have imagined. I took my wedding ring off. I took it off to fit in, and in that moment I didn't feel good about my choice, but I was determined to fit in. The guys I was with were picking up women, and I didn't want to be the guy who blocked their mission. So I removed my ring, and I talked to some girls, and then I went back to watching basketball. I know it was dumb.

I came home from that trip to Vegas, and I could feel the weight of that choice on my shoulders. I had wronged my wife, and now that feeling was coming between the two of us. My dishonesty had put an emotional wedge in my marriage. The only thing I could do was come clean. After several days, we sat down and had the tough conversation. There were tears, there was anger, but at the end of it all our relationship was better because of it.

I realized that bad news doesn't get better with age, and the longer I waited to have honesty in our relationship the more harm I was doing. Honesty promotes open communication and trust, both of which are priceless commodities when doing life with the person you love.

Prayer

Lord, you are the way and the truth and the life. Help me live in truth, your truth. Please help me be completely honest with my spouse. Help me share everything going on in my mind and heart and lay it all out there to him or her even if it seems ridiculous in my head. I pray that my spouse would also be honest with me and that I would be receptive to the ideas and feelings he or she shares with me. Help me love regardless of what I hear. Help me be a committed and truthful spouse for the long haul.

III. Individual Journal Questions

1. Is there anything in your life you are hiding from your mate? Read Genesis 3:1-13. Why did Adam and Eve hide from God? Are there similar reasons we don't share everything with our spouse?

2. In the story of Eric and Julia, what is one thing you know your mate would not understand if they found it out? Is there any way you could bring this up the next time you talk to him or her?

3. What do we lose by being honest? Think over the story Tony tells in the "True Confessions" section. Have you ever done anything like Tony did in Vegas? Have you told your spouse about it? Do you gain more or less respect by not being honest? Write down an example of when you have hidden something from someone else to gain his or her respect.

IV. Couple Interactive Exercise

Unbreakable Skill #2: The Communication Accelerator Method (CAM)

CAM involves a simple exercise between two people.[1] It can happen on the spur of the moment but usually works best when time is set apart for a deeper discussion, like on a date night.

CAM involves one person starting the conversation by explaining fully what is on his or her mind. The other person listens without interrupting until the first person has reached a good stopping point.

The second person then repeats back what was just said to him or her without comment. This gives the first person feedback about what was actually communicated to his or her partner. After a full summary has been delivered, the first person

---

1. CAM is a technique adapted from the Speaker Listener Technique from PREP Inc. (https://www.prepinc.com/). We learned this technique while in the Army.

again gets the opportunity to rephrase himself or herself so what was meant becomes what is actually heard. The second person will make another effort to summarize what the first person just communicated. This is only half of CAM.

Next, the second person is allowed to speak uninterrupted for a length of time, and then the first person has to repeat back what was said. If not understood exactly right, the second person gets to rephrase his or her feelings and allow the first person to try to understand again. Couples can then continue to use CAM for the rest of their time together by each taking turns speaking. It usually works best to have something the speaker can hold, like a relay baton, or even a pencil, to designate who is supposed to be talking.

With CAM you keep the important issues on the forefront and allow each person to be fully heard and feel honored. It is not easy to allow someone else to talk for a length of time when what he or she is saying may not be 100 percent accurate. However, CAM permits the second person to have the same uninterrupted opportunity, and he or she can certainly comment on what the first person said. If the conversation ever gets too heated, then taking a time out is an acceptable method to get over the hump.

Couple Exercise

Practice the Communication Accelerator Method (CAM) for a while on a topic that is not too controversial (see suggestions below). First, have the wife begin with a topic, then have the husband begin.

Rules for the Speaker (S)	Rules for the Listener (L)
S-Speak only for yourself	**L**-Focus on what is being said without interrupting
S-Use "I" statements like, "I felt sad when . . ."	**L**-Paraphrase the speaker during each pause
S-Don't talk on and on	**L**-Don't argue with the speaker
S-Stop after each statement so the listener can paraphrase	**L**-Show respect and be polite

Suggested topics: dream vacation, dream job, kids' achievements, what makes your favorite movie so good. Until you practice, avoid finances, in-laws, physical intimacy, and so on.

V. Couple Questions for Date Night

1. Decide together on two topics that usually end in conflict when you discuss them. What are the sticky points? Why does it infuriate one or both of you?

Try using CAM on one of these issues, and see if you can move past the negativity and get to the fruit. There is usually a hidden issue with most contentious topics.

2. How is the story of Eric and Julia like your relationship? How is it different?

3. Have you ever lost a friend by being too honest with them? Is there a time when you shouldn't be honest with those you love?

4. What is one way you can increase honesty in your marriage relationship?

5. Reflect on something your spouse needs to hear from you tonight (to bring clarity and closure) and tell him or her.

VI. Small-Group Study and Discussion Questions

1. **Open** in prayer.

2. **Ask:** Why is it important to have honesty in a relationship?

3. **Read** out loud the background story.

4. **Ask**: In what ways is your marriage like Eric and Julia's?

5. **Read** 1 Corinthians 13:6, "[Love] is happy with the truth," and Ephesians 4:15.

6. **Ask:** What is the connection between love and truth? Can you think of other places in scripture where these two ideas are combined? Why would Paul write that love "is happy" with the truth? Is honesty that important in relationships? In the Ephesians verse, what is the connection between love and maturity? What does God's love have to do with honesty?

7. **Review** the "True Confessions" section. Have you ever done anything like Tony did in Vegas? What was the end result?

8. **Ask:** Is there anything holding you back from having a closer marriage with 100 percent honesty?

9. **Close** in prayer after asking if anyone else has something they would like to share with the group about honesty in their marriage.

VII. Unbreakable Challenge

Make a commitment to not tell your spouse a lie, a fib, or even shade the truth a hair for the next five days. Commit that everything you say is exactly the way you see it in your heart and mind—without sugarcoating. Expect some rephrasing; you might be amazed how often we struggle with this.

Develop a marriage promise statement for honesty by filling in the blank below:
*I promise that I will*_____
_____.

Unbreakable Love Concept #4— Forgiveness

Be kind, compassionate, and forgiving to each other, in the same way God forgave you in Christ.

—Ephesians 4:32

Main Point

Forgiveness is not letting someone off the hook. It is not forgetting. It is not an emotion or a feeling. Forgiveness is an action step someone takes because he or she loves another person. It is willingly letting go of resentment and the right to get even. It is allowing the other person to be accountable to God for his or her actions and allowing oneself to love him or her through difficulties. Forgiveness is unilateral.

I. Background Story

"Not again," cried Sarah when Ryan stumbled into the house with red, swollen eyes and alcohol on his breath.

Grabbing the front of his coat with both hands, she shouted, "Why do you do this to us?"

Before Ryan could respond, Sarah ran to the bedroom bathroom and shut the door behind her. She needed to cry and wanted to be alone.

Ryan is an Army MP (military police) recently returned from an overseas deployment. Since returning home, Ryan had been coming home from work late more often each week. When Sarah confronted him about it, he agreed to change and only see his platoon buddies one night a week. This week, however, he had gone out after his shift for three nights in a row, on his way back from the fort. Ryan was always quick to apologize but slow to change his behavior. Sarah was not sure she could continue on in the marriage; this was not what she signed up for. The deployment was hard enough, but when he returned home, his newfound coping mechanism was almost too much for Sarah to bear.

Ryan took off his boots and made his way into their bedroom. He knew the kids had been bathed, read to, prayed with, and tucked in for the night, all without him being home. Ryan had failed Sarah again, and he wasn't sure how much longer she would put up with him. He knew he needed to change, but he just couldn't get his act together. When he left work, he had every intention of driving straight home, but then he felt the ache to drink and relax for a while. Their family life was a little stressful with young children, and after a long day at work it was just too hard to go home some nights.

Ryan sat down with his back against the bathroom door. He knew it was locked; he didn't even have to try the handle. He brought his knees up to his chest and wrapped his arms around his legs. The next thing he knew he woke up to Sarah speaking to him through the door.

"Are you there, Ryan?" she asked. "I can hear you snoring."

"Yes, honey, I'm here." Ryan rubbed his eyes. He felt like a two-time loser. He couldn't even stay awake to talk to his wife and apologize before he fell asleep. She had done all the bedtime chores with the kids, and he couldn't even keep his eyes open for a few minutes to apologize. *How long had I been asleep?* he wondered.

"I'm mad, and I couldn't deal with you when you got home," Sarah said.

"Yes, honey, I know. I'm sorry I fell asleep."

"You're pathetic, you know that?"

"Yes, hon. I know it."

"Ryan, we're not going to do this anymore."

There was a long pause with neither of them speaking. Ryan knew he had blown it, and he kept thinking of past times he had let Sarah down. He couldn't understand why she was still with him.

"Honey, I'm sorry. I meant to come home tonight but I—" Ryan didn't finish his sentence. Nothing he could say would excuse his behavior and he knew it.

"Ryan, I'm not sure I know who you are anymore. You don't fight for your family—you avoid us. Plus, you spend money on alcohol when I can't even buy everything I need for the house and the kids. You know that Jimmy needs new shoes for basketball? How much did you spend this week at the bar?"

"I'm not sure, Sarah. I can't think straight at the present moment. I agree with you, though. You're right. I'm not fighting for our family." Ryan was resisting the urge to go back to sleep. He couldn't keep his eyes open.

"I think we need to go to counseling," Sarah said. She was glad Ryan was listening and agreeing with her that he had a problem. Sometimes he would just go to bed and gloss over everything in the morning.

"How much would that cost?" asked Ryan, not really believing counseling was the answer.

"It doesn't matter, Ryan. I think it's cheaper than other alternatives."

Ryan knew what she meant by that. In a past argument they had talked of separating or divorce yet knew it would destroy both of them financially. Through it all, Ryan believed he had been a good father to his kids, despite his unwillingness to change his nighttime behavior. *I don't need counseling*, he thought. *I just need to change my behavior and quit going to the bar.*

"Will you be able to forget about tonight so we can start over?" Ryan asked. His eyes were closed and his forehead was resting on the top of his knees. He was really hoping she would say yes.

There was a long pause, and then Ryan heard the door open, almost causing him to fall backward on the tile floor.

Ryan turned around and saw Sarah on her knees, just two feet away from him. She was in a white nightgown, and she looked so beautiful to Ryan, like an angel.

Sarah reached over, put both her hands on Ryan's cheeks, and, holding his head steady, she locked eyes with him.

"No, Ryan. I cannot forget about tonight. You have a problem, and you need to get help. However, I have forgiven you. I made a decision even before you got home that whatever time you arrived, and in whatever condition, I would forgive you with all my heart. I just needed a moment alone to recommit myself to that after I saw you. I forgive you, Ryan, for everything."

Ryan couldn't speak. His eyes welled with tears. "I'm so sorry. I'm so sorry." He reached up to hug her, but she held him at arm's length.

"Ryan, you need to listen to something. I forgave you, and I will do it again. However, together we are going to work on getting you help. I am not going to enable you any longer." After saying that, Sarah gave Ryan a hug, and they cried together.

II. Going Deeper

The Scriptures

"If you forgive others their sins, your heavenly Father will also forgive you. But if you don't forgive others, neither will your Father forgive your sins." (Matthew 6:14-15)

"Watch yourselves! If your brother or sister sins, warn them to stop. If they change their hearts and lives, forgive them. Even if someone sins against you seven times in one day and returns to you seven times and says, 'I am changing my ways,' you must forgive that person." (Luke 17:3-4)

"Brothers and sisters, if a person is caught doing something wrong, you who are spiritual should restore someone like this with a spirit of gentleness. Watch out for yourselves so you won't be tempted too." (Galatians 6:1)

"Be tolerant with each other and, if someone has a complaint against anyone, forgive each other. As the Lord forgave you, so also forgive each other." (Colossians 3:13)

The Principle

Jesus makes it clear in the New Testament that it is absolutely essential to forgive others as God has forgiven us. Horizontal (humans with humans) and vertical (God with humans) forgiveness are not incidental. Jesus taught that human forgiveness and God's forgiveness are inseparable. When a person claims to have received unmerited forgiveness from God but doesn't forgive another, he or she denies the reality of his or her own faith. The kind of love you need to forgive originates from God. Human love cannot fully forgive an enemy. Human love has limits. It takes a spiritual power to move past ourselves and give a gift like forgiveness to another person. It takes an alternative strength to forgive an enemy. This inward strength of character is love, and this love comes from God.

Arrows on Target

Because of our self-centeredness, we are going to repeatedly hurt our mate, and he or she is going to hurt us. This is why couples have to learn about forgiveness and practice it often. Because forgiveness is a unilateral activity, we are not to hold out for a soft heart in another because it may never happen. We need to move forward, be a person of action, and forgive others from the heart. This is radical love. This brings unforgettable fire into a relationship.

Whoever told you forgiveness would be comforting or help you sleep better at night was dead wrong. God does not forgive us in order to sleep better at night. God forgives us as a gift of love for us and demands that we forgive one another from the heart.

When you and your husband or wife came together, you said you would be there for each other through thick and thin. When betrayed, it is close to impossible to forgive the betrayer; but when broken by another, there is an alternative strength to assist us, the spirit of God.

Do not wish for a perfect marriage. Marriage is the place to find reality, not an ideal. In marriage you find out what people are made of. When an offense is committed, it causes a divide. One member of the couple must get past the need to get his or her own way, to be "right," or to feed his or her own ego. One person of the couple has to move forward with love so deep it plants seed to bloom again.

True Confessions

(Tony speaking) I am a jerk. I am mean and manipulative, and sometimes I don't treat the people I love very well. Asking for forgiveness is something that I do on a pretty regular basis in my relationships. Too often my brokenness shows through, and I do something (or fail to do something) that hurts my wife.

In 2007 that hurt came in the form of pornography. I was on an army deployment in combat away from my wife, and it started to creep in on me. At first it was because I was lonely, then it was because I was bored, and finally it was because I "needed" it. I was hurting my most important relationship on earth. In addition to hurting Karen, I was also not living in the calling that God wanted for me. Then, in a moment's notice, it all came crashing down. Literally, my computer crashed. I was going to have to get it fixed and tell my wife about the porn in the process.

Let me assure you that there is no easy way to tell your wife that you're hooked on pornography. There is no easy way to say that you've been secretly hurting her and that you need forgiveness. Lucky for me, Karen showed me that forgiveness, and in addition to that we worked together on a plan of restoration. Forgiveness is the first step in restoring wholeness, and it means admitting that what you were doing was wrong. Asking for forgiveness requires humility and is something that shouldn't be taken lightly. However, when you receive forgiveness, it can be like lifting one thousand pounds off your shoulders. It is the first step in restoring sanity to your pain and requires nothing short of the grace of God.

Prayer

Lord, who is a God like you who pardons sins and forgives the transgressions of his people? You do not stay angry forever but delight to show mercy to your people. Please help me be more like you. Help me not count offenses and be a quick forgiver. Help me show a radical love to my spouse even when he or she hurts me. Help me not be angry and bitter with my spouse, and help me be honest about my own offenses. Help my sweetheart know how much I love him or her. Open our eyes to the reality of your forgiveness and grace to us, and help us show that same grace to each other.

III. Individual Journal Questions

1. When you think about forgiveness and your relationships, whom do you need to forgive? What areas of your own life do you need forgiveness for? Have you forgiven yourself?

2. In the story of Ryan and Sarah, could you relate to one of them because of your spouse's actions? Read Colossians 3:13. Write down some things that you are bearing and some things your spouse is bearing for you.

3. Read again what Tony wrote in "True Confessions." Consider whether there is something in your life that would devastate your spouse if made public. How can you prayerfully prepare yourself for a discussion about forgiveness? Write a prayer to God in the space below.

IV. Couple Interactive Exercises

Unbreakable Skill #3: "Forgiveness Steps"

When you know you have wronged your spouse and you need to ask for forgiveness, you can follow these steps below:

1. Completely own the wrong in your mind.

2. Confess the sin to God.

3. Ask for strength and power to overcome future temptation in this area.

4. State the offense to your spouse, without minimalizing, and say you are sorry.

5. Genuinely apologize and own that you have hurt your mate deeply.

6. Ask for forgiveness. Discuss what behaviors you will change to ensure the offense will not happen again.

7. Reaffirm your love for your spouse, and work with him or her to rebuild trust and change.

When your spouse has wronged you and he or she comes to you and asks for forgiveness, you can follow these steps below:

1. Pray trusting God will settle all scores, and do not seek revenge (see Romans 12:19).

2. Pray to God that you will not hold resentment and be bitter.

3. Forgive your spouse fully and out loud to him or her.

4. Seek to understand your spouse.

5. Work with your spouse to restore trust in your marriage and help him or her to change.

Exercise #1

Reflect on these questions privately and write your answers:

1. What prevents me from forgiving my spouse?

2. What would I give up if I forgave?

3. What does God think when I don't forgive?

4. What do I do about the hurt I might still feel?

5. In what ways do I take things too personally?

6. Why is it hard to admit my own guilt?

Exercise #2

Think of several ways you have hurt your spouse or violated his or her trust in the past. Write them down in the first column. Think of several ways your spouse has hurt you or violated your trust. Write them down in the second column. Place a star next to the items that were truly devastating. Place an "F" next to each item in the right column that *you* have forgiven fully. Discuss these lists with your spouse either now or this week during your couple meeting.

How I **Have Hurt My Spouse**	**How My** **Spouse Has Hurt Me**
_____	_____
_____	_____
_____	_____
_____	_____

V. Couple Questions for Date Night

1. Review both sets of answers in exercise #1 of the couple interactive exercises. Were any of them similar?

2. Have you ever had to deal with a situation like Tony shared in "True Confessions"? Are you stronger because of this?

3. Have you ever had a friend come and ask for your forgiveness? What was the outcome?

4. What is one way you can increase forgiveness in your marriage relationship?

5. Reflect on something your spouse needs to hear from you tonight (to bring clarity and closure) and tell him or her.

VI. Small-Group Study and Discussion Questions

1. **Open** in prayer.

2. **Ask:** Why is it important to have forgiveness in a relationship?

3. **Read** out loud the background story.

4. **Ask:** In what ways is your marriage like Ryan and Sarah's? Did you grow up in a home where forgiveness was practiced? How did this pattern impact your own marriage today?

5. **Read** the four different scripture verses in the "Going Deeper" section.

6. **Ask:** Do these commands of Christ go against human nature? Why or why

not? What does Paul mean in Galatians to be careful that you are not tempted when you restore someone (6:1)?

7. **Review** the "True Confessions" section. Is there a story like Tony's you are comfortable sharing with the entire group? Make sure you have your spouse's permission first!

8. **Work together:** If you haven't completed the couple interactive exercises yet in section IV, do them now. Did you learn anything new about your spouse in exercise #1?

9. **Study** Ephesians 4:32. What is the relationship between kindness and forgiveness?

10. **Close** in prayer after asking if anyone else has something they would like to share with the group about forgiveness in their marriage. Give an opportunity for individuals in the group to think about forgiveness with each other as well.

VII. Unbreakable Challenge

One night this week, before the end of the evening, hold hands and kneel beside the bed (side by side). Have each person take a turn at reading the prayer out loud in section II, "Going Deeper." Then, if needed, use the "Forgiveness Steps" listed in the couple interactive exercises section.

Develop a marriage promise statement for forgiveness by filling in the blank below:
*I promise that I will*_____
_____.

Unbreakable Love Concept #5— Sacrifice

*Love puts up with all things, trusts in all things,
hopes for all things, endures all things.*

—1 Corinthians 13:7

Main Point

With shallow love we seek possession, and we dwell on what should be returned to us. With sacrificial love we give part of ourselves away and allow the other person to transform into someone we cannot control. This takes vulnerability, and it is hard to embrace this kind of openness and exposure. But when we're vulnerable and open is when we're most powerful. Being there for our spouse when absolutely no one else on earth can be—that's sacrifice. Knowing all of his or her faults, weaknesses, and bad habits, yet still wanting to spend time with him or her—that's sacrifice. Doing things for him or her without pay back—that is the currency of sacrifice! Sacrifice is the highest form of love. It is not appeasement, acceptance, or pandering; it is an action step, a decision, a passage.

I. Background Story

One night before bed, Tim and Helena found themselves on the sofa beside their fireplace holding hands and looking at a catalogue together.

"Tim, I need to tell you something," said Helena suddenly.

"Okay, fire away," said Tim.

"I want to go back to work. I know when we first started our family that I was the one who wanted to stay home with the kids. Making this place our home has been meaningful for me for a long time, but things are different now. The kids are all in school and self-sufficient. Our oldest has a driver's license to get the family around if we're not home. And I have the desire to use my degree and get back into the workplace. I know there will be some obstacles, and things might feel different around the house, but I have a plan for that. If I get up extra early and spend time on weekends catching up, you and the kids will hardly know I'm away during the weekdays."

Tim breathed out and looked straight ahead. He had known this conversation would come back up; he just didn't know it would be tonight. He definitely had reservations about Helena going back to work, but he knew she had put her career on hold to raise the family. She had done a great job with the kids. She deserved something more if she wanted it.

"Helena, I'm okay with it. You've been in the home now for over fifteen years and have done a great job of raising the kids. I think you should go back to work, if that would make you happy."

"Really? Oh, thanks, Tim. I am so glad you feel that way."

The couple embraced, and then Helena immediately started looking online for a job matching her skill set.

In a few weeks Helena found a job and began working regular hours during the week. The first thing Tim noticed with Helena's absence was that the house was a little messier in the evening when he came home from work. Also, sometimes the bed wasn't made and Helena's pajamas were on the bathroom floor. *Well, she's in a rush in the morning; she's only been on the job for a few days*, Tim thought.

As the weeks went on, there were other things that began to bother Tim. At first Helena made an effort to prepare meals ahead of time, on weekends, in an effort to provide a hot meal for supper during the week. But over time, her weekends became busier with kid's activities and she was pretty tired from working all week. Though they were excited when her first couple of paychecks came in, Tim soon found he was spending much more money for food at restaurants for takeout.

One Saturday morning, after a few months with Helena working, Tim looked around the house and noticed kids' schoolwork scattered across the living room and dining room, along with clothes and miscellaneous locker items. He walked into the kitchen and found a pile of dishes that had accumulated during the week since last Sunday when he personally cleaned the kitchen. Tim walked back into their bedroom where Helena was still sleeping, and he noticed her clothes strewn around the floor, outfits she had or hadn't worn laying on the bed and the desk and chair. Helena was so exhausted each weekend that they hadn't made love for two weeks. He wanted to wake her up to be intimate, but she was sleeping so soundly, he didn't dare.

Tim walked back into the kitchen and ran a basin full of water. He would clean the kitchen, and then have a talk with Helena.

Later never came. Three more weeks went by, and things hadn't changed in the house. In addition, the kids' assignments weren't being signed and returned so their grades were suffering. Laundry was stacking up around the house, and no one's bed sheets had been changed in months. There were a couple of items needing repair in the house, but since no one was home during the day to let the repairman inside, the work was left undone. Helena was more irritable around the family and spent more time on the phone texting her new friends at work.

Tim sat down on the sofa in the quiet house that Saturday morning. He was mad. He was doing more grocery shopping, along with more vacuuming and more dishes than he ever had in his life. *What kind of life is this?* Tim wondered. When Helena got up, he was going to have it out with her.

He then decided to pray and read his Bible for a little bit. What immediately jumped out at him was a verse from the Gospel of John where Jesus said, "This is my commandment: love each other just as I have loved you" (John 15:12). Tim pondered this verse for a moment. He thought about how much Christ loved him, so much so that he died for him. Tim rethought about all that was wrong in the house and how his own needs weren't being met. Then he thought about Helena and how many years she had taken care of the house. He experienced a deeper appreciation for her efforts now that he had to assume some of those responsibilities. In many ways, she had sacrificed much more for the family than he ever had.

Tim prayed and asked God to change his attitude toward his wife. He then made a decision. He decided he would try loving Helena sacrificially, by doing things for her without expecting anything in return. He would clean the dishes and not get mad. He would straighten up the living room and not be bitter or complain about it. He would make sure the kids' school assignments were completed and turned in each week. *Besides, why should she have to do all the same work? She is away from the house just as much as I am. If I am going to be behind Helena and support her through her new work experience, then I need to change my attitude*, he thought.

Tim was still cleaning the house when Helena came out of the bedroom looking for her first cup of coffee.

"Hey, honey, why are you working so hard on a Saturday morning?" she asked. "You ought to go back to bed and get some rest."

"That's okay," Tim responded. "I have a few more projects I want to get done around the house before the kids get up. How did you sleep, sweetheart?"

"I slept well. Thanks for being such a great husband."

Helena walked over to Tim and gave him a big hug. Tim hugged her back, and they held each other for a moment.

"Helena, I'm sorry I've been a grumpy with you lately and not supportive. I know you have a lot on your plate now with work and the kids and everything. I realized this morning that I have been resisting your efforts to keep the family going by not jumping in each night when I get home. I let things build up, and then I get angry at you, and that's not fair. I need to help you more, and I'm sure we can do this together if we both pitch in. I love you, honey. Thanks for being a great wife."

Tears came to Helena's eyes. She felt appreciated and understood by her husband for the first time in a long while.

II. Going Deeper

The Scriptures

"This is my commandment: love each other just as I have loved you. No one has greater love than to give up one's life for one's friends." (John 15:12-13)

"Therefore, imitate God like dearly loved children. Live your life with love, following the example of Christ, who loved us and gave himself for us. He was a sacrificial offering that smelled sweet to God." (Ephesians 5:1-2)

"For example, wives should submit to their husbands as if to the Lord. . . . As for husbands, love your wives just like Christ loved the church and gave himself for her." (Ephesians 5:22, 25)

"This is love: it is not that we loved God but that he loved us and sent his Son as the sacrifice that deals with our sins." (1 John 4:10)

The Principle

Sacrifice is the pinnacle of love because it is demonstrable love. Like forgiveness, it is an action and takes work. It is the picture of a soldier giving his all for his country, or an athlete foregoing all pleasures in life in order to compete like a champion. It is also the picture of a marriage when the sacred duty of love invites itself upon a spouse to bear everything.

This is the kind of love that communicates to others they are more important than anything. The kind of love that communicates above all else I did it for you. As you see in the triangle, commitment is love's base, but sacrifice is the pinnacle expression of love. It allows individuals to perform Christlike actions for another. Though only one initiates the action, it dives a couple into the bottomless pool of revitalizing and thirst-quenching love.

Arrows on Target

A sacrifice is a relinquishing of something at less than its value. God did this for us through Jesus. In ancient society gifts were given to gods on the outright basis of *do ut des*, "I give that you may give," a favor for a favor. Christ was different. He gave all he had to those who could do nothing for him. Jesus surrendered himself for others to gain. In the process he lavished us with God's love.

Couples can bring sacrificial love into their marriage as well. For instance, when a spouse has a disability or is terminal and needs his or her lover to assist and care for him or her in ways he or she never thought imaginable at the beginning, they both experience a foretaste of heaven. With the right attitude, a sacrifice of this nature propels this couple into *agape*, an unconditional love.

Being there for someone when he or she most needs you and can't give anything in return—that is sacrifice. Missionaries who give much of their salaries and savings to the people they minister to—that is sacrifice. Giving your spouse a lifesaving experience, such as protecting her from danger, or providing an organ for him to live—that is sacrifice. It is not *quid pro quo*, this for that. It is not society's "what have you done for me lately?" mentality.

Unfortunately, many couples never reach this stage. We swim in a society with mediocre images of marriage. Divorce is a knee-jerk reaction, and self-centeredness produces stalemates before the supreme acts of loving sacrifice have a chance to occur.

Sacrificial love makes one vulnerable. It is an experience in which one commits to the uncommitted, loves the unlovable, forgives the unforgivable, and desires the beloved's good simply for the beloved's sake. It is quite exposing.

True Confessions

(Karen speaking) I married Tony knowing that he was in the army, so I guess I thought I knew what my sacrifices for marriage would be. I figured that being a soldier meant he would have to travel; I would have never guessed he would be gone a whole year. In retrospect, what I realized is that sacrifice has to be 100/100 (not 50/50). We both have to sacrifice in order for this marriage to work. There is no middle ground on this topic; if we both aren't willing to sacrifice, then it just won't work.

The hardest part for me about sacrifice is the resentment. Yes, we are both sacrificing, but it feels like Tony always gets to do more fun stuff while I am at home by myself. His responsibilities are more for just him, while I have to be the one to juggle everything at home. The other difficult part about sacrificing as a military spouse is that I don't get a say in what he does or when he leaves. It sometimes feels like I have to give up what I personally want to do so that I can be home with the children. I guess the easiest way to say it is that in the event both of us have something to do, Tony's mission takes precedence (whether I like it or not). Even when Tony is home, I sacrifice my personal agenda so that I can be with him or have family time. When Tony is gone I miss out on those times, so when he is home I take advantage of it and it becomes my priority.

Sacrifice is important for me because it is the outward display of my commitment to the marriage. As a spouse I get to sacrifice for my family so that we have unity in our world. While it's not always easy, it is something that I am going to have to do if I want to be in this marriage. My husband is committed to the army and his vocation. As a pastor's wife I sometimes feel like I have to show daily sacrifice because there is always someone, something, or some ministry that bumps ahead. When those moments happen, I have to be really careful about my attitude so that I can stay supportive rather than turning into the resentment queen. Two of the things I do in order to stay in a positive place are prayer and open communication with my husband about how I'm feeling. One thing I know about myself is that if I don't unload those feelings of resentment, I will explode like a volcano. I love talking to him about my life, because at the end of the day, it is one of the things that I need to do in order to keep going.

Solid communication is a tool that helps make sacrifice more manageable, but I don't ever forget that it's still hard. If it were easy, it wouldn't be sacrifice.

Prayer

Lord, you have shown us the greatest act of sacrificial love by putting to death your innocent son so that we sinners might live. Please help me think of ways that I can sacrificially love my spouse. Help me be there for him or her when he or she needs me most. May I get out of the habit of wanting something returned to me when I do something for my spouse. Help use my life as an offering for my spouse and for others around me. I want to give boldly and live a life filled with love, following the example of Christ, who offered himself as a sacrifice for us. Please, Lord, give me the strength to make this happen.

III. Individual Journal Questions

1. Write down two ways you have sacrificed for your spouse. Write down two ways your spouse has sacrificed for you. How much time does each sacrifice take? Are some shorter than others?

2. Reflect on the story of Tim and Helena. Write down ways that Tim sacrificed for the family. Write down ways that Helena sacrificed. Should Tim have been upset?

3. Read Ephesians 5:1-2. What does Paul mean by living your life with love? Write down a way you could live your life with love in your home and at work.

4. In Karen's "True Confessions" story, what was Karen's biggest source of resentment? What are some ways she handled her situation so she wouldn't explode? What are the ways you respond when you feel resentment toward your spouse? Is there a certain perspective you could have to mitigate the feelings of resentment with your spouse?

IV. Couple Interactive Exercises

Exercise #1

Read each sentence below and circle the corresponding letter. Circle "A" for always, "F" for frequently, "S" for sometimes, and "N" for never.

1. I believe in my spouse.	A	F	S	N
2. My spouse believes in me.	A	F	S	N
3. I accept my spouse for who he or she is.	A	F	S	N
4. My spouse accepts me for who I am.	A	F	S	N
5. I sacrifice for my spouse.	A	F	S	N
6. My spouse sacrifices for me.	A	F	S	N
7. I work hard at being a loving spouse.	A	F	S	N
8. My spouse works hard at loving me.	A	F	S	N
9. My spouse knows that he or she is my top priority.	A	F	S	N
10. I know that I am my spouse's top priority.	A	F	S	N

11. I verbalize honor and respect to my spouse.　　A　F　S　N

12. My spouse verbalizes honor and respect to me.　　A　F　S　N

13. I really see my spouse's needs and respond to them.　A　F　S　N

14. My spouse really sees my needs and responds to them.　A　F　S　N

Exercise #2

Think of a time when your spouse sacrificed for you and made you feel wonderful. Write or draw what he or she did and how you felt at the time.

Think of a time when you sacrificed for your spouse. Write or draw what you did and how he or she felt at the time.

V. Couple Questions for Date Night

1. Provide for each other a definition of sacrifice. Does your definition fit into a marriage context? Does it fit into your marriage?

2. Think about what you are currently sacrificing in your marriage? Is there resentment there that you need to let go of?

3. Sacrifice is an act of love. What is something that you need to sacrifice for the greater good of your marriage?

4. How is the story of Tim and Helena like your marriage? How is it different?

5. Share an example of when your mate displayed the love of sacrifice to you. How did it make you feel?

6. Take time to just say thanks to your spouse for sacrificing what he or she has already given up.

VI. Small-Group Study and Discussion Questions

1. **Open** in prayer.

2. **Ask:** Why is it important to have sacrifice in a relationship?

3. **Read** out loud the background story.

4. **Ask:** In what ways is your marriage like Tim and Helena's?

5. **Read** out loud Ephesians 5:22-32.

6. **Ask:** What is the connection between marriage love and Christ's love for the church? How can a husband love his wife as much as his own body? Does this even make sense? Many people struggle with this passage. It raises good questions and elicits healthy discussion about how we are to serve and minister to one another in healthy and equal relationships. To you, what does it mean for a wife to submit to her husband (v. 22)? How does this relate to sacrifice? What kind of submission is appropriate in marriage? What kind of submission and sacrifice is *not* appropriate in your marriage? What are ways that husbands can love their wives with sacrificial love? What are ways that wives can demonstrate respect for their husbands? How are these commands like a two-way street?

7. **Review** the "True Confessions" section. Have you ever had to sacrifice for your spouse when you didn't want to or had no say in it? What was the end result?

8. **Work together:** If you haven't completed the couple interactive exercises yet in section IV, do them now. Did you learn anything new about your spouse in exercise #1?

9. **Close** in prayer after asking if anyone else has something they would like to share with the group about sacrifice in their marriage.

VII. Unbreakable Challenge

Decide on one big, audacious idea that allows you to sacrifice for your spouse this month. What is one super thing you could do that he or she wouldn't expect and for which there is nothing he or she could do to pay you back? Don't do it just to get ahead of your spouse and compete, but offer your sacrifice to him or her as a gift of love. Think of who he or she is and what he or she likes or needs right now. It might involve spending money by providing a trip. It might involve many hours of your time to serve him or her. Whatever you decide, commit to it with pure motives and provide it as a gift.

Develop a marriage promise statement for sacrifice by filling in the blank below: *I promise that I will*_____
_____.

Author Note for Sessions 2–6

We have tried to teach you about a love not tied to the other person's actions as much as it is tied to your own Christianity and God's love pouring through you. One tag line for this marriage curriculum might be: *to discover and give the deep love of God to your spouse.* This process is about loving your spouse with the intense love of God. It is a formula that will never fail you, even when your spouse doesn't play by the same rules or read the same books.

Through these lessons you have learned about following God's *hesed*, loving-kindness (from the Old Testament), and Christ's example of sacrifice (from the New Testament). This kind of love can put an unforgettable fire into any relationship. With commitment, kindness, honesty, forgiveness, and sacrifice, we are becoming better Christians and truer to the vows we made in our marriage, even if our spouse is unable or unwilling to reciprocate. We must change ourselves, our own hearts, and modify our own behaviors. And we must turn off the desire to change our spouse. Each person is responsible for his or her own self and reactions. Instead, dwell on the biblical truth that God is making us new through Christ. You have pledged to love your spouse powerfully; sometimes this will cause you to cry. Strive not for a heart unbroken but for a love unbreakable.

Togetherness

I belong to my lover,
and his longing is only for me.
Come, my love:
Let's go out to the field
and rest all night among the flowering henna.
Let's set out early for the vineyards.
We will see if the vines have budded
and the blossoms opened,
see if the pomegranates have bloomed.
There I'll give my loving to you.

—*Song of Songs 7:10-12*

Main Point

Marriage—at its best and as God intends it—is a source of deep and unfathomable love. It is a reflection of God's relationship with humankind through Christ. A beautiful minuet is danced by those who see this beauty and allow God to help them weave their marriage tapestry into a picture of the love of God. You've got gaps. Your spouse has gaps. Fitted together you may look and act more like God, and this is a mystery, a glimpse given to two people of the holiness of God.

I. Background Story

Duke and Katie had been married for twenty-two years. They had four children, all girls, and the oldest one was a freshman in college. What Duke desired the most was time alone with Katie. What Katie desired the most was time to herself.

Katie was a stay-at-home mom and seemed to always be at work with laundry, cooking, dishes, or cleaning. When she finally got some free time to herself, one of the girls would need a ride somewhere or Duke would want to make love to her.

One Saturday night in late summer, three of the girls were out of the house, and the youngest one was in the basement watching television with her dad. After Katie finished cleaning the kitchen, she called her sister and talked for a while. Then she sat on the sofa thinking about how nice it would be to go to bed early. Suddenly, Duke came up from the basement and, eyeing Katie on the sofa, made his way to her side and began rubbing her feet.

"I was thinking of going to bed early," said Katie.

"That sounds good to me," said Duke.

In a few minutes they had finished their bathroom rituals and were under the covers with the lights out. In the darkness they could hear from the basement the television just below them.

After a moment of silence, Duke rolled to his side, facing Katie, and began to give her a back rub.

"That feels good, Duke, thank you. How was your day?"

"Fine, the usual stuff at work. I'm glad tomorrow's Saturday and we can sleep in a little bit. Do you know where the girls are?" Duke kept rubbing Katie's back, neck, and arms.

"Oh, that feels great," said Katie. "The girls are over at Rhonda's house watching a movie. They shouldn't be home for at least another hour."

"That's perfect," said Duke.

"Perfect for what?" asked Katie.

"What do you mean, 'Perfect for what?' You know what I mean."

"Duke, didn't I tell you I'm pretty tired tonight?"

"Yes, but when you said, 'Let's go to bed early,' I thought that meant Duke-and-Katie time," responded a hopeful Duke.

"Duke, I didn't go to bed early so we could make love together. I went to bed early because I'm tired after a long week of working in this house."

There was an awkward silence for a moment, and Duke didn't know if he should keep rubbing or not. He decided he should continue because there was always hope.

After a couple of minutes Duke said, "Katie, I know you're tired, but would you mind giving in tonight to help me out? It's been a few days since we've had time together."

"No, Duke, I'm tired. I've told you three times now. I don't have the energy to make love with you tonight. Maybe if you had helped me in the kitchen instead of going downstairs to watch TV after supper, things might be different. Please don't ask again."

Duke was stung by this comment. He decided it was time to stop rubbing. On one level he was glad he knew the final answer and it wasn't a guessing game any longer. On another level he was irritated that she brought up that he had not helped her with the dishes. It was definitely a rebuke, and it hurt a little bit.

"So I have a question for you," said Katie.

"What's that?" asked Duke, somewhat relieved she wasn't giving him the silent treatment.

Just then their door sprang open flooding the room with the hall light.

"Mom, are you taking me to soccer practice tomorrow?" It was their youngest daughter.

"Yes, dear."

"What time is it?"

"I think it's at nine thirty."

"What time do we need to leave?"

Duke was getting annoyed with all the questions and the light invading their bedroom. He rolled over and faced the other side of the room.

"We need to leave around nine fifteen, honey," responded Katie.

"Okay, will you call me at eight forty-five?"

"Yes, honey."

"Oh, Mom, we don't have any Gatorade. Could we leave early so we can stop at the store and get some?"

"Sure."

"Now what time do we need to leave?"

"Um, about nine."

"Okay, call me at eight thirty."

"Okay, honey."

"Goodnight, Mom."

"Goodnight, honey."

"Love you."

"Love you too, sweetheart."

Finally the door closed, and the room was dark again. Duke was wondering why their daughter didn't say goodnight to him as well. Then he remembered Katie was asking him something.

"What were you saying, honey?" asked Duke as nicely as he could to mask his massive disappointment with not having sex that night.

"My question is—I was wondering if you rubbed my back just because you wanted to make love tonight?" Katie asked.

"No, of course not. I thought you needed a back rub."

"But why? I didn't say my back was hurting me."

"I just thought so. Can't I do something nice for my wife once in a while?" Duke was sounding a little put out.

"I think you were doing it just because you wanted sex. You often do that, Duke. Most nights you come to bed and go right to sleep as if I'm not even here. But nights you want sex you start talking to me and rubbing my back."

"So what's wrong with that?" Duke asked as he rolled back over to face her direction. He wasn't really following her logic, though he thought she might be insinuating something.

Just then, the front door opened and slammed shut. Their two middle daughters returned home for the evening.

"I just think you cuddle up to me only to get your needs met. Sometimes I would like some nonsexual affection from you. You only touch me when you want my body."

"That's not true. I mean, I always want sex, so what am I supposed to do, not ever touch you?"

"No, you're missing my point, Duke."

Suddenly the door flew open again, flooding the room with light.

"Good grief, kids!" bellowed Duke. "Don't you ever knock?"

"Oops, sorry, Dad." It was their second youngest daughter. "Just wanted to check with Ma to see when my piano lesson is tomorrow."

"Just knock next time, that's all," said Duke, rolling back over to face the wall again.

"I'm pretty sure it's at eight tomorrow, honey, but you will have to check on my calendar in the kitchen," answered Katie to the original question.

"Well, Caroline said she was sleeping in and couldn't give me a ride tomorrow. Do you mind waking me up at seven thirty?"

"No, honey, I don't mind. Just please check the calendar to make sure."

"Okay, goodnight, folks."

"Goodnight," answered Katie.

Duke didn't respond, but he was glad he was remembered this time.

"Now what were you saying?" asked Duke.

"I don't remember," answered Katie. "But I'm really tired. Do you mind if we talk about it tomorrow?"

Just then the door sprang open again.

"You're right, Mom. It's at eight. Wake me at seven thirty, okay?"

"All right, honey."

"Goodnight, Mom."

"Goodnight, sweetheart."

There was a moment of quiet until the television was turned on again in the basement. Duke was lying on his back, wondering if there was going to be any more discussion about sex tonight. Then he was wondering why he forgot to lock their bedroom door. Soon he began to snore.

"Duke, you're snoring. Roll over."

"Oh, sorry. Hey, we went to bed early tonight. Why are you so tired, anyway?" Duke asked.

"I don't know. I just hit a wall once I sat on the sofa. Fatigue from the day kind of crept up on me. We'll talk more tomorrow. I just want you to be a little more considerate. I need cuddle time once in a while without sex."

Their bedroom door opened up for the fourth time. It was Caroline.

"Hey, Mom. Sorry I can't do the drop off for her piano lesson. I have a sleepover tomorrow night, so I really need my rest tonight. Do you mind driving her to her lesson?"

"No, honey. It's okay, I'll drive her."

"Thanks, Mom. Have a good night."

"What about me, Caroline? I'm here too."

"Oh, hey, Dad, sorry. Goodnight."

The door closed, and there was darkness once again.

Duke rolled over, away from Katie, and said, "I still don't understand why you're always so tired."

II. Going Deeper

The Scriptures

"I'm a rose of the Sharon plain,
a lily of the valleys.
Like a lily among thornbushes,
so is my dearest among the young women.
Like an apple tree among the wild trees,
so is my love among the young men.
In his shade I take pleasure in sitting,
and his fruit is sweet to my taste.
He has brought me to the house of wine;
his banner raised over me is love." (Song of Songs 2:1-4)

"The husband should meet his wife's sexual needs, and the wife should do the same for her husband. The wife doesn't have authority over her own body, but the husband does. Likewise, the husband doesn't have authority over his own body, but the wife does. Don't refuse to meet each other's needs unless you both agree for a short period of time to devote yourselves to prayer. Then come back together again so that Satan might not tempt you because of your lack of self-control." (1 Corinthians 7:3-5)

The Principle

There are three types of togetherness. There is time as a couple in public (like taking a walk, going to the store, or going to the movies together). There is time as a couple in private but nonsexual (like cuddle time or watching television together). And, there is time as a couple in physical intimacy. It is important for married couples to remember that all three times are important: casual time, cuddle time, and under-the-covers time. When casual time or cuddle time is eliminated from the relationship, the wife often begins to be unhappy. When the sexual time is eliminated, then the husband becomes unhappy. The important piece to remember is that there needs to be balance for both to be happy. Most men need sex (more than women) to feel loved and appreciated. Most women need casual time and cuddling to feel loved and cared for. The couple that can strike a balance will be happy for the long haul.

Arrows on Target

Every person alive today struggles with the same disease: selfishness. It becomes easy to react to others with a "what have you done for me lately?" attitude. Selfishness slowly enters every marriage like an invader and constantly captures more territory. Either we recognize and stop its demands, or it conquers us. No one likes to live with a tyrant. However, with this invasion the danger to marriage is not primarily destruction, but stalemate.

There is absolutely no one who you will find a problem-free relationship with. Sure, some couples are more compatible than others, but everyone has to deal with his or her selfishness to succeed in marriage. Hollywood will never tell you that. The notion that there is a "right" person out there who will be effortless to live with is pure moonshine.

Sometimes it seems that love in marriage is too much work. Some ask, "Wouldn't it be better to live a single life with lots of partners?" This scenario may sound enticing, but it would not be fulfilling for very long. Any of God's creatures can treat each other with carelessness and one-night stands, but we are image bearers. We humans were made in the image of God, unlike the animals in God's creation. As such we are God's image-bearers, meant to reflect the love of our creator. Marriage—at its best and as God intends it—is a source of deep and unfathomable love. It is a reflection of God's relationship with humankind through Christ. You've got gaps. Your spouse has gaps. Fitted together you may look and act more like God, and this is a mystery, a glance given two people of the holiness of God.

True Confessions

(Charles speaking) My physical relationship with Lauri has seen its ups and downs. Overall, Lauri has been wonderful to me in this area. There have been many nights when I have gone to bed and not said a word to her, and she still loves me. There have been many nights when I haven't cuddled her, and she still made love with me. On most days I realize the gift I have in her, but it hasn't always been easy.

There was a period of time when, for some reason, I felt I needed more and more sex. It was during our time in seminary, and I kept pushing her to initiate intimacy with me and not say no to me so easily when I initiated. I am not sure why, but for a period of two years it seemed that sex was always on my mind.

When this period was over, Lauri shared with me that she had been struggling with post-partum depression, and it was a very dark time for her. I asked her why she didn't tell me and help me see how hard that era was for her. She told me that she knew I was having a tough time going to graduate school full time while working two jobs to support our family. She said she wanted to be strong for me. I wept when I heard this.

I would make love to my wife every night if she desired. Lauri is wired to be happy with a little less. We've had to balance my need for sex and her need for intimacy. What my wife needs most from me is nonsexual affection. For my wife, intimacy is an all-day event, not an intermission. It is something that builds for her throughout the day. I have to create the mood by my actions all day long, not just with a back rub when the lights go out. This forces me to be a better Christian and to be loving and gentle and thoughtful when dealing with my spouse. I also have to realize that this is what is expected whether there is intimacy in the bedroom or not.

In the same way, if Lauri expects intimacy with me, she can't simply wait until those times when she is excited to respond to me. She needs to be there for me sometimes, even when she could just as easily go to sleep. One thing Lauri does for me that I appreciate is say, "Charles, I can't now, but how about we take a nap tomorrow during lunch?" Even though it feels like I am close to death at that point, it helps, and then I can look forward to it. Knowing the negotiating is complete and we will have sex in the next 24 hours, I can relax. She doesn't say next week or next month, and she also doesn't say maybe later—but later. It is helpful to a husband's state of mind to know he doesn't have to start from scratch.

The longer I've been married to Lauri, the deeper I fall in love with her. The deeper I fall in love with her, the more I see my selfishness. The more I see my selfishness, the deeper I experience the love of God. My relationship with Lauri has been my great advantage. In marriage, I have seen God.

Prayer

Lord, you are the maker of both sexes. You designed sexual intercourse to be mutually pleasing to the husband and the wife. Thank you for this great gift to married couples. Empower me to love my spouse in the way he or she feels most loved. Help me meet my mate's intimacy needs first. Help me grow in depth of understanding in how to please my spouse. Help us be creative and flexible and have fun in the bedroom. You created this part of our lives, so we trust you to provide a path for us to enjoy it.

III. Individual Journal Questions

1. Do you invite God to be a part of your physical intimacy? Why or why not? Are you willing to honor God in your physical relationship with your spouse by prayer and open discussion? Take a moment now to write a prayer to God on this issue.

2. What are your sexual expectations with your spouse? Do you openly discuss them with him or her, or do you secretly resent your spouse for not meeting your needs? Write down what you think would be an ideal sexual relationship.

3. In most relationships there is a partner who craves physical affection while the other partner has less of a need for this. Which partner are you? Are you actively meeting your spouse's need or just focusing on what you want? Read the background story from section I. Are you more like Duke or Katie?

IV. Couple Interactive Exercises

Exercise #1

Physical intimacy is a divine blessing to married couples and a gift from God that is designed for pleasure. A satisfying marriage relationship grows best when couples combine both sensuality/cuddling and sex in the majority of their moments of physical intimacy. Divvy up the circle into three parts based on your current relationship: The amount of physical intimacy with sex but without sensuality/cuddling, the amount of physical intimacy with sensuality/cuddling but without sex, and the amount of physical intimacy where both sensuality/cuddling and sex are present. Look at the example before you begin.

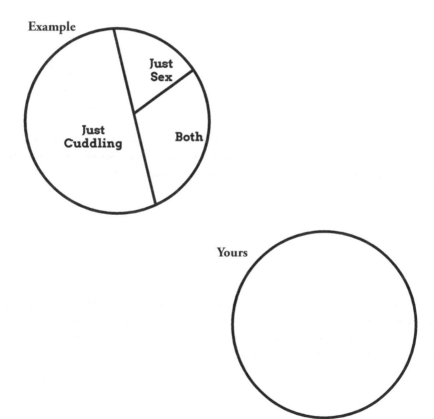

Exercise #2

How satisfied are you with the physical relationship you experience with your spouse? Circle the number that corresponds to your answer.

Satisfaction with...	Low → High
the level of respect your spouse shows you in the bedroom	1 2 3 4 5 6 7
the level of creativity/variety you experience in the bedroom	1 2 3 4 5 6 7
the frequency of physical intimacy you experience in the bedroom	1 2 3 4 5 6 7
the level of care and tenderness experienced during lovemaking	1 2 3 4 5 6 7
the level of passion experienced during lovemaking	1 2 3 4 5 6 7
the ability to speak with each other about your lovemaking	1 2 3 4 5 6 7
the overall happiness of your physical relationship	1 2 3 4 5 6 7

V. Couple Questions for Date Night

1. As a couple, review the circles you drew in exercise #1. Discuss why the lines were drawn the way they were and what an ideal circle might look like.

2. As a couple, go over your results from exercise #2. On which questions were your answers the most similar? On which questions were your answers the farthest apart? Discuss ways to improve your relationship in areas you would like to grown in.

3. Discuss physical intimacy and your marriage. Are you both happy with where it is, or do you need to improve in an area?

4. Discuss emotional intimacy in your marriage. Are you doing the necessary emotional work to promote physical intimacy?

5. Read Song of Songs 2:1-4 together and discuss its meaning. Share with your spouse your favorite part about the physical intimacy you share.

6. What can you do to promote the habit of dating your spouse? What dates can you put on the calendar right now?

7. Romance is something that is refined over time. Share with your spouse what you need romantically from him or her at this point in your life.

VI. Small-Group Study and Discussion Questions

1. **Open** in prayer.

2. **Ask:** What is your favorite memory of time spent with your spouse?

3. **Read** out loud the background story.

4. **Ask:** In what ways is your marriage like Duke and Katie's?

5. **Read** 1 Corinthians 7:3-5.

6. **Ask:** Why do you think Paul wrote this passage? Is it possible to defraud your mate of what is rightfully due them?

7. **Read** Song of Songs 5:10-16 and 7:1-9.

8. **Ask:** What stands out to you in these passages? Would it be right to say that sex is a gift from God and designed for our pleasure? Then why is it so hard for some couples to make it work?

9. **Review** the "True Confessions" section. Have you ever had a period of time where physical intimacy was challenging? What was the end result?

10. **Close** in prayer after asking if anyone else has something they would like to share with the group about intimacy in their marriage.

VII. Unbreakable Challenge

Plan a getaway for a weekend together. If it is financially possible, reserve a hotel room for at least two nights. (If not, make arrangements to get away at a friend's cabin, a low-cost retreat center, or some other option away from home.) Plan to stay in bed together one of the days. Bring food and beverages with you for that day, and eat it your room. Or order room service! If possible, don't bring your cell phones (or keep them turned off once you check in).

Develop a marriage promise statement for togetherness and physical intimacy by filling in the blank below:

*I promise that I will*_____

_____.

Putting It All Together

Notice the five unbreakable love concepts in the pyramid. Write in the promises section (below) your seven promises (one from each session), then put it all together and develop a marriage mission statement. A marriage mission statement is a goal, purpose statement, or covenant you intend to keep as the years progress. An example might look something like this: *My mission is to live the love pyramid and display commitment, kindness, honesty, forgiveness, and sacrifice to my spouse on a daily basis to develop a legendary love with him or her!*

1. I promise that I will —(foundations)—

2. I promise that I will—(commitment)—

3. I promise that I will—(kindness)—

4. I promise that I will—(honesty)—

5. I promise that I will—(forgiveness)—

6. I promise that I will—(sacrifice)—

7. I promise that I will—(togetherness)—

My Marriage Mission Statement:

The Love Vow

Congratulations. You have finished *UnBreakable* and are on the path toward deeper love with your spouse. Before you put this book on a shelf, consider taking the love vow below with your spouse. This can either be done with your small group (if you went through the *Unbreakable* curriculum with others) or alone as a couple. Take a moment to hold hands, look into each other's eyes, and vow these five promises to each other.

—I will keep my word and be committed to you for a lifetime.

—I will show undeserved kindness to you and accept responsibility for my own actions.

—I will listen and be completely honest with you.

—I will grant unilateral forgiveness and seek reconciliation with you when an offense occurs.

—I will act sacrificially whenever our relationship needs me to.

I, _____, vow these five things to you, _____, as long as we both shall live!

Date: _____

Postscript: The Story behind *UnBreakable*

Tony and I had just finished leading a marriage conference for sixty couples at an elite conference center in Chicago. It couldn't have gone better. Marriages were strengthened; couples fell in love again; we laughed a lot and had a great time together. Even the food that weekend was extra tasty. As we packed our bags around noon on Sunday—the conference having just ended—Tony received a call on his cell phone from a very distressed spouse. She told him that before they left their hotel room her husband ended their marriage and declared he wanted a divorce. Tony told her to wait right there and to keep her husband from leaving. He then came to my room, and we both ran down the hallway searching for the couple's suite. When we entered their hotel room, there was heavy tension in the air and no one was saying a word. It was frosty. Their bags were packed, and they were each sitting on opposite sides of the room. Needless to say, our pride was a little hurt after having just invested two days into this couple's relationship, only to have it end up in a worse state than it was when they arrived. But sometimes that happens. The issues we bring up and the skills we teach enable couples to speak about things that really matter to them.

For this couple, the husband finally verbalized that he really did not like his wife or want to be around her. Some things she had done in the past made it impossible for him to forgive her and move on. To say that Tony and I felt this was an opportunity for crisis counseling would be an understatement. I'm not sure what Tony was thinking in that instant, but it seemed my next few words would decide the fate of this family, that their marriage was hanging on a thread tied to my tongue. I did not know where to start. Honestly, I cannot remember all we talked about, but I know we entered into a discussion with them about their early days and what drew them together. We talked about a love, deep down, that wasn't expressing itself. We talked about what they learned at the conference and what triggered this fracture before they left. We talked about some of the love principles in this workbook. In the end, they promised to spend more time talking together and working on their marriage. They had our phone numbers with privilege to call 24/7.

After a good ninety-minute delay, Tony and I were walking back to our rooms to retrieve our luggage so we could check out. In that moment we both experienced a powerful sense of God's presence and knew what our lives needed to be about. We shared with that couple everything we had to offer about faith, hope, love, and being committed to a partner you can't always understand. Simply put, in that moment we sought to pour our lives into the couple. This marriage workbook you're holding is also an outpouring of our lives. It was written with the hope that each couple journeying through it would understand more fully the love of God and would develop a deeper love for their mate, striving not for a heart unbroken but for a love unbreakable.

The Biblical Basis for the Five
Core Components of Love

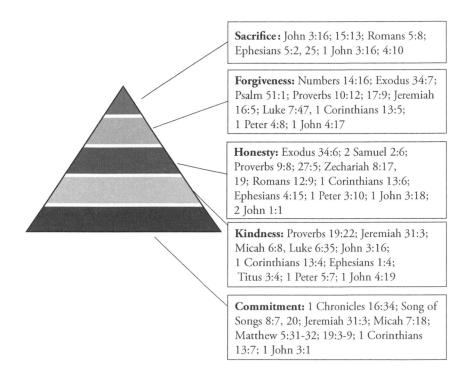

Sacrifice: John 3:16; 15:13; Romans 5:8; Ephesians 5:2, 25; 1 John 3:16; 4:10

Forgiveness: Numbers 14:16; Exodus 34:7; Psalm 51:1; Proverbs 10:12; 17:9; Jeremiah 16:5; Luke 7:47, 1 Corinthians 13:5; 1 Peter 4:8; 1 John 4:17

Honesty: Exodus 34:6; 2 Samuel 2:6; Proverbs 9:8; 27:5; Zechariah 8:17, 19; Romans 12:9; 1 Corinthians 13:6; Ephesians 4:15; 1 Peter 3:10; 1 John 3:18; 2 John 1:1

Kindness: Proverbs 19:22; Jeremiah 31:3; Micah 6:8, Luke 6:35; John 3:16; 1 Corinthians 13:4; Ephesians 1:4; Titus 3:4; 1 Peter 5:7; 1 John 4:19

Commitment: 1 Chronicles 16:34; Song of Songs 8:7, 20; Jeremiah 31:3; Micah 7:18; Matthew 5:31-32; 19:3-9; 1 Corinthians 13:7; 1 John 3:1

*For a more complete understanding of *UnBreakable* from a biblical perspective, read Charles Causey's doctoral dissertation entitled "A Victory of Love."

Acknowledgments

From Tony

The following individuals and groups helped make *UnBreakable* possible:

Our amazing friends and family who had to constantly hear us rambling about the book

Ginghamsburg Church (www.ginghamsburg.org)

Jason Moore and Midnight Oil Productions (www.midnightoilproductions .com)

From Both

Our agent Dan Balow and Connie Stella, Kelsey Spinnato, and the rest of the Abingdon team.

From Charles

A big thanks to the congregation of Crossway Fellowship in Manassas for allowing us to conduct a pilot marriage class with this material and specifically the fifteen couples who participated. This group included Alan and Candy Cole and Robert and Kim Payne, who helped Lauri and me with the teaching. The writings of C. S. Lewis and Dietrich Bonhoeffer had a part in my understanding of love, as did my seminary advisors who stimulated and challenged me—Loyd Melton (Erskine), Scott Manetsch, and D. A. Carson (both at Trinity). Other important people who shaped my thinking on relationships over the last twenty-five years were these mentors: Bill Bright, Robert Coleman, Bill Culbertson, Henry Foster, Dean Johnson, Joe McKeon, Bob Nieuwendorp, Doug Rietema, Steve Simpson, and George Wold. The marriage of Keith and Nanci Davy inspired me at the beginning, and the marriage of

Acknowledgments

Mark and Christine Tatum (our current small-group leaders) at the end. This book is not only dedicated to my wife; it also blossomed out of my love relationship with her. I cannot express enough how much Lauri means to me, but these few Shakespearean lines from *The Merchant of Venice* are a good start:

> *For she is wise if I can judge of her.*
> *And fair she is, if that mine eyes be true.*
> *And true she is, as she hath proved herself.*
> *And therefore, like herself—wise, fair and true—*
> *Shall she be placed in my constant soul.*

CPSIA information can be obtained at www.ICGtesting.com
Printed in the USA
LVOW01s1940110714

393963LV00004B/5/P